Transcendence – My Rebirth as a Woman
Nikki DiCaro

Nikki DiCaro

Notice

Mention of specific people. organizations, or authorities in this book does not imply endorsement by the author or publisher, nor does mention of specific people, organizations or authorities imply they endorse this book, its author or the publisher.

Requests for information should be directed to:
DiCaro Consulting
Attention: Nikki DiCaro
www.nikkidicaro.com
nikki@dicaro1.com

To Benjamin and Felicia
Thank you for unconditionally accepting me and loving me without regard
for what's on the outside. You have truly inspired me to be the best person
I can be.
I love you so much!

Introduction

I'm Nikki DiCaro. I'm a successful business executive and a published author. I've raised four children (not alone) and have a gaggle of grandchildren. I'm a blogger, frequent speaker, coach, consultant and facilitator. I'm an entrepreneur. I love to dance, cook, exercise and meet people. I'm all these things and I'm also a transwoman. I'm about to take you on a journey of discovery. This journey was long, arduous and sometimes harrowing. Fear, trepidation, anxiety, expectation, anticipation, dread and hopefulness accompanied me along the way. My emotional world could become overcrowded!

Like many people, I have bouts of doubt. My moods and outlook change depending upon the events that transpire. I love to think I have control over things in my life. I'm here to tell you that's probably more illusion than reality. You will learn the uplifting power of love and friendship and the destructive force of rejection coming from those who profited most from my life's work.

This series, Transcendence, is an ongoing writing experience in which I bare my soul and hopefully provide valuable insights into my world, including the world of gender dysphoria and transgender. But this isn't one of those dramatic, woe is me, stories. Sure, you'll have the opportunity to see the world through my lens. It's sometimes cloudy and other times clear. I'll share my emotional struggles. I'm sure they're not unlike some of the mountains you've climbed and the demons you've slayed along your journey.

I'm presenting these memoirs in installments; each will focus on a segment of my life. There's no right or wrong order to reading them. Each installment will be unique and I'm sure you'll connect with them at some level.

Over the past ten years I've discovered the power of the written word. It has freed me. Writing has allowed me the opportunity to memorialize thought, to compartmentalize fear, to rally inner strength. Most importantly, writing has granted me the privilege to reach people where they are and hopefully instill hope and confidence when reservoirs were dangerously low.

These memoirs are about my life, my journey, my struggles and my triumphs. I hope you will read them, absorb them and reflect upon them. Not for me, but for you. Learn about the struggles of gender dysphoria. Understand this ailment afflicts many people. How many is unclear since we don't have an accurate count of the transgender population because this population is counted through self-identifying. Transgenders don't freely self-identify. Stigma and fear around admitting to living with gender dysphoria keeps people in the shadows; hiding their authentic self, locked in the depths of themselves.

No person should be relegated to hiding; not even hiding in plain sight. Because the energy expended during the struggle is wasted and can never be recovered. Hiding can be destructive and devastating to the sufferer. That's one of the reasons the suicide rate among transgenders is eight times – that's right 8X – the national average. Any suicide is bad. It deprives the victim and every life the victim touched, from experiencing beauty and fullness. Suicide leaves a void, an unfillable emptiness and miles of regret in its destructive wake.

If you're on the fence about transgenders or if you're biased or have pre-judged (prejudice comes from lack of knowledge or understanding) us, I hope my journey will help you see us as we are, human beings just like you. We bleed red and our money is green. What else do you need to know in order to realize we're you, and we're carrying a very heavy burden we didn't choose.

These volumes will vividly display struggles, setbacks, fears and finally redemption.

Thank you for reading. Please reach out to me through my website if you have questions or need help.

Chapter 1

Exiting the vehicle on the sidewalk side of the street I felt lightheaded. I couldn't believe I had reached this point in my journey. Four years passed in the blink of an eye. Here I was, standing before the biggest decision of my life and I was exhausted from lack of sleep and overnight activities that weren't for the faint of heart.

I hadn't eaten in more than thirty-two hours; unless you count bowls of chicken broth and ginger ale as sustenance. On top of that, my regimen of drinking water had been upended. No fluids after midnight; doctor's orders. This was the gauntlet I was required to run if I was going to see this part of my transition through to completion.

Memories of drinking those salty, slimy prescription beverages that do unnatural things to you made me realize I had passed another milepost on this incredible journey. Up all night dealing with the masochistic results of bowel prep I wondered if this was all worth the sacrifice. It was as if the preparation was designed to get you mentally conditioned to run to get the thing over and done. I dismissed the voice in my head that tried to convince me to stop at the gift shop for something to eat or drink, anything to make the hollowness in my stomach disappear and clear the fog that hung lazily over my brain. If you've ever had a colonoscopy, you feel my pain.

The hospital entrance, on a traffic-clogged main artery in Philadelphia, PA bustled with morning activity. Eight-thirty a.m. approached and shifts were changing with factory efficiency. I wondered if any of these people were going to be members of the surgical team to assist in my physical transformation.

Retrieving my roll aboard suitcase from the trunk of the SUV, my friend handed it over before hugging me and wishing me much success. Tom had recently undergone hernia surgery that left him hobbling through recovery. He was a saint to drag himself and his lady, Mary, out of bed on a dreary and damp December morning to chauffeur me to the hospital. I watched them pull away as I stood on the sidewalk, foot traffic oblivious to the firing of nerve endings as conflicting signals raced to my brain.

Lingering a long moment, I tried to comprehend the magnitude of today's adventure.

Tucking the strap of my handbag over my shoulder I grabbed the extended handle on the rolling luggage and turned toward destiny. I shook off the thought and melted into the pedestrians entering the hospital. Walking through the main entry I crossed the point of return; the invisible line between dreams and reality. The sense that something big was about to transpire hung in the air like morning mist coming off an active ocean. The guard at the front desk pointed me towards the elevators, the long run of hard surface, a veneer of manmade materials that had been scrubbed and buffed. The floor seemed to reflect latent concerns that were overpowered by the growling of my stomach.

Turning, the first step seemed light; as if my feet were devoid of feeling. Surreal; an out of body experience. Was this really happening? The culmination of years of waiting, wishing and hoping came down to this. The long walk seemed even longer with each step, the wheels of my suitcase clicked in unison with my stride.

The prior day was a blur. Obligatory surgical preparation robbed me of two worldly pleasures; eating and sleeping. Weakness from lack of food and water – I began to understand the beginnings of a forced hunger strike. I wore no makeup. I didn't feel naked; maybe I was dreaming this. My hair was covered by a cloth cap; one of my stylish and expensive wigs tucked lovingly in my suitcase. "After this part of my transformation is complete I'll address building a luxurious head of high maintenance hair," I told myself as I walked.

Reaching the bank of elevators I stopped; standing among a phalanx of cisgender women; my sisters. I wasn't certain the look on their faces was the joy of another day of work or trying to figure out why the newest addition to the gathering was wearing a head wrap. A mixture of awe and trepidation struck me hard. No makeup, no food, no liquids, no problem – all part of surgery prep – seemed to fuel mild delusion. It felt like all eyes were upon me; my heart lying bare. I needed to keep moving forward to prevent doubt from shifting my transmission into reverse.

Entering the elevator, I tried to focus on the journey and the reason I felt okay with venturing into the unknown – no real fear or trepidation. I expected excitement; anticipation. I was preparing for the longest step in my journey; one from which there was no physical return. Was I ready? I've been asking that question for years; not for lack of confidence. I analyzed each step towards every milepost. So far, not one goal unreachable nor unachievable. But this one required more than all the others combined. I was attempting something that was unusual and by conventional standards, unnatural. The unknown opened before me. Uncharted territory. A yawning portal, my version of the looking glass. *There's no return from this one Alice. Welcome! The door swings one way!*

Pushing the button for the ninth floor I counted as the cab stopped at each floor. Passengers exited and others entered. I began to wonder if this was another of the vivid dreams that had colored the landscape of sleep over the past three weeks since I signed up for this mission to the land of physical womanhood.

Stepping off the elevator on the ninth floor I hesitated. A hitch in my step, a pause of uncertainty. "Last chance to turn and run. It's not too late. Are you really sure you're ready for this? You could always call a cab." The voice in my head tested me. Forging on I continued the trek towards destiny. A nurse greeted me and directed me towards a small room with two large recliners and an overbed table. Taking a seat I waited. More time to contemplate. I recalled all the videos I watched and all the information I read about Vaginoplasty, et al. I dismissed the thoughts as nothing more than churning of psychological butter.

My belongings were positioned on a second chair. I over packed but I still felt like I had forgotten something. Even after all those years of business travel, hundreds of thousands of air miles and I had forgotten the art of packing efficiently; unsure what I would need during my brief two-day visit. An orderly stopped by to deliver clean, well-worn surgical garments, the ones that left little to the imagination. I wasn't going to be adorning the cover of any magazine in these; except maybe *Physician's Weekly* or *Surgery and Sutures*. Stripping off each article of street clothes drove home the reality of my surroundings. The little voice, the one that had been clamoring for a major reality check, echoed from the depths of my subconscious. "You're cold and hungry and maybe a little crazy. Why are you doing this?"

"Because it's what I want."

"Are you really sure? Maybe you're off your nut. Speaking of nuts, how's your stomach?"

"Yes, I'm sure. About my stomach, let's not go there," I answered firmly with the loudest mental voice I could muster. There was silence for a long moment.

"Remember those videos you watched? Remember how you clutched yourself to ward off the threat of pain and a long traumatic recovery?"

"Yes, I remember. But I'm going to be fine. If others could do it, I could too." I tried to convince myself this was right and I was ready. I began to wonder if I was talking out loud. Hunger will play those tricks.

The voice relented; blessed mental silence! Shaking off the last remnants of trepidation I slipped on the two surgical gowns, one open in the front and the other open in the back. Then came the hospital socks with the traction strips on the bottom. I felt naked and vulnerable but not alone. Instead I felt surrounded by supportive people. This was my surgeon's hospital; a teaching hospital.

Three nurses came by to check on me, ask questions, maybe see if I was drawing on the walls or clutching at the air to catch imaginary butterflies. Eventually one nurse would be responsible for logging all of my information. I thought I felt something in the air; almost like peace was settling over me to assure this decision was not only permanent but more importantly correct for all the right reasons.

I engaged the intake nurse in conversation. We struck up a friendship; not one that appeared superficial. I didn't feel like she was obliged to be kind and considerate. I felt I made another connection on December 7, 2016. She promised to stay in touch. I knew her promise was filled to overflowing with compassion. She sensed I needed a friend at my most vulnerable time. She was right. Nurses who work with the infirm and surgery candidates know. Nobody can do this for you. I've heard the phrase 'everybody dies alone.' The same is true for surgery, even as all the well-wishers lined up to assure me I was going to be fine. I was there

9

alone with all of my thoughts and feelings. That's a moment when you know you're human; a moment that really tests your inner strength.

Recalling conversations with my five closest friends, a couple of them feigned jealousy; labeling me with the "B" word for jumping to the front of the line. The statements were followed by warm words of encouragement and we laughed together. The memories helped to tamp down the confluence of thoughts and emotions that crashed into each other.

The two most important days of your life are the day you were born and the day you found out why. – Mark Twain

I sat in the oversized vinyl-covered recliner; my legs propped on the roll aboard luggage, my coat across my body to keep warm. It seemed I was always cold since starting hormone regimen eighteen months ago. I guess I was experiencing my personal Autumn. The intake nurse brought a blanket and plastic bags to hold my belongings that didn't fit in the suitcase; offering to show how to recline the chair. I must not have looked comfortable. She was a veteran professional; I wasn't the first transgender she had seen. That helped drain the tension from the air. Her voice was soft and comforting as if making me comfortable would somehow tame the thoughts that vied for time with my inner voices.

Awaiting the call to surgery I continued to contemplate what was about to transpire. I had done more reflecting, more evaluating and more imagining over the prior three weeks than I had done prior to my coming out. I'm a person who likes to have enough information to make a decision. I was committing to a physical change some people coveted and most people didn't or wouldn't comprehend or understand. I was exchanging male genitals (my junk or my package as it was affectionately labeled) for female genitalia. I tried to imagine the outcome; attempting to apply business acumen to this situation. How would I feel afterwards? Would I really leap for joy at seeing myself as I had imagined for almost half a century? My body's going to undergo a physical change. My psyche is also going to undergo a cataclysmic change. Should I be scared? I marshaled bravado; reminding myself I didn't come this far to turn back.

I thrive on knowing the outcome; measuring from data collected from others. But their journey was tangential to mine. Were they mentally and physically stronger or weaker than me? Should I worry about the post-surgical complications some had bemoaned? Should I let others influence me; cloud the sky over my moment in the sun? My transition was discovery – every moment of every day another revelation. I decided to block all that information. They were data points and not necessarily facts directly applicable to my circumstances.

I processed what others had said or written. What had I learned from many years of research, investment, success and failure? Collecting information should be performed with due care and a healthy dose of skepticism. There's as much information as there is misinformation about procedures and outcomes. Also, it's not easy to quantify the variables of health, activity, diet, sensitivity to pain, medical history, etc. on a person's ability to handle and accept the consequences of a decision. Every decision or indecision, action or failure to act carried consequences. I had made peace long ago that I would accept consequences of my decisions. I knew what I wanted to accomplish. The wait that seemed eternal was about to end. I knew one thing for sure; there most likely would be post-surgical pain and at least six weeks of recovery. At my age recovery was more likely to be six months! I was willing to take the risk to live for one day in the body I had craved for all those years.

Chapter 2

Nurses came and nurses went; the flurry of morning activity in full swing. I sat contemplating; I had been doing much reflecting. That happened when I was alone with my thoughts and the voice of reason and the voice of wishes, hopes and dreams echoed in my head. I was adventurous; never backing down. I welcomed challenges and change. This adventure, the resultant change, was going to eclipse anything I had experienced.

Music infiltrated my mind; the calming sound of James Taylor reminded. The authentic me – Sweet Baby James had a way of reaching me; reminding me the length of the journey. The journey of discovery was filled with wonders and the thrill of avoiding every pothole and negotiating every speed hump. I wanted this change as much as I wanted anything. This change would not define me. It would affirm me. All those times before the mirror, standing naked in a way that hid the appendage that the world uses to define maleness, tucked away to present the illusion of a female body below the waist. "I can do this," I affirmed almost out loud.

James Taylor's words spoke as much of me as to me. She's around me now. She's been around me for years. Various authors and songwriters have speculated on the meaning of the words in this song. Rolling Stone critic Jon Landau regards the song as being about "transcendence of a sort."[i] Author Barry Alan Farber used "Something in the Way She Moves" as one of his favorite songs on the theme of love that "both comforts and strengthens."[ii]

Songs, words penned by artists sending a message of trying to find their anchor, their tie line, their connection to the world. Some never do. The same can be said for people. Life has a strange way of offering momentary comforts along a road sometimes shortened by inexplicable events. Mine was no different. I was a nomad. I was searching even when I didn't know it. I wandered through life, touching down from time to time until restlessness grabbed me and pulled me to my feet. Songs touched me deeply. I enjoyed the melody but preferred songs whose words were more than a compilation of rhymes. I could be moved deeply by the right combination of words and inflections. James Taylor's music had a way of touching me beyond other artists. His journey of discovery was fraught with many times of uncertainty. I felt that maybe his music was meant to help me.

Recalling four years of transgender journeying, I realized I emerged from the feeling of loneliness and isolation when I discovered the local transgender community through an on-line group. Over Fifty years of my life, half a century, had passed at a frenetic pace when the first markings on the map of my journey materialized. Today marked two years, ten months and twenty-five days since Nikki emerged from the shadows of worry cutting and hacking through the bramble of isolation. It wasn't until I made my inaugural public appearance that I realized I wasn't alone. I wasn't going to allow myself to become a member of the "Failure to Act" club.

The call came. "Are you ready for surgery? They're calling for you." The few steps from the waiting room to the hallway seemed to cause my stomach to bottom out. "This is happening. I mean this is really happening!"

Climbing onto the gurney another bang of the reality gavel. I was heading towards destiny, the impact of post-surgery and the long road to recovery. Was I really ready to bid adieu to an appendage I had known for fifty-eight years? The voice of reason reminded it wasn't too late to step away from the gurney and rethink this voyage into uncharted territory.

The orderly greeted me. The man was kindly; his demeanor projected many years of work wheeling surgery candidates to the operating room. We chatted. His warmth and gentleness added an air of calm to the hint of nerves that threatened to blossom into concern; the flowers of terror their petals sharp and unforgiving.

The surgery preparation area bustled. People in scrubs scurried from patient to patient. Nurses approached and asked the obligatory questions. My gastrointestinal tract rumbled and complained. The prior day's bowel preparation made me appreciate my health and reminded that I was hungry and thirsty.

The anesthesiologist made several attempts to insert an intravenous junction connection into my left hand. He apologized as we chatted.

Three attempts and he relented. A nurse tried my right hand. The first attempt a success.

I'm a worrier; concerned about a lower GI accident during surgery. "I have to go to the bathroom," I announced to the nearest nurse. Helping myself off the gurney I stood with the help of one of the male nurses.

Striding towards the bathroom I felt the room spin. My vision grayed nanoseconds before I collapsed. My prior gender identity would have labeled it a blackout. My authentic gender correctly labeled it a fainting spell.

The next thing I remembered was lying on the gurney, my legs elevated by one of the nurses. I was weak and vulnerable. "Is this how the aftermath of a spiked drink felt?" Dread crept over me. The surgeon approached. Maybe I wasn't meant to have the procedure. Maybe this was the wakeup call. *She's not getting our messages. Time to send in the big guns!*

"Am I going to be able to have surgery?" I asked, presuming I was headed home; unsure whether to worry or rejoice.

"Full speed ahead. This happens all the time." The nurse said as she connected a saline drip to the intravenous port.

The surgeon looked at me, her eyes soft and a smile on her lips. I expected her to override the nurse and send me home. *So sorry Nikki. We can't risk surgery with you in this weakened state. Call my office and let's reschedule you when you're stronger.*

"Doc, what's this mean?"

"This happens all the time. After what we put you through; no food or water, this isn't unusual. We're almost ready for surgery. Are you ready?"

"I was born ready." I said enthusiastically; my patented line. The surgeon smiled, reassuring me. The saline drip nudged back the lightheadedness that felled me moments ago.

When humanity changes from hating people's differences to accepting and learning from humanity's differences, that's when we'll become a civilized society. – anonymous

The call came and I was wheeled into the operating room. Was I in a daze and oblivious to what was about to transpire? I didn't feel anything; no fear or trepidation, no anxiety but also no excitement. I had made the decision. Probably more accurately fate or the universe, had positioned me here on this day at this time for a purpose greater than anything I could imagine. There are things larger than I sometimes have the capacity to understand. I wrestle with trying to figure things out or letting them ride as I travel along a road upon which I am sometimes only the passenger of a vehicle being driven by fate. The road will take me where I am destined to go. My role appears to boil down to being open to whatever the universe, or fate, has in store for me.

Chapter 3

This struggle started when I turned thirty. It wasn't a lightning bolt that jarred the normalcy or scrambled the electrons that moved aimlessly searching for positive electrical charges to pull them into a patterned orbit. It started slowly at first. I began to wonder about life. Was there a hidden meaning? Was I supposed to keep turning over rocks until I found a message? At thirty I seemed to cross an invisible barrier. The great continental divide of my journey. Age is only a number. I believe that more and more as I continue to add digits to my life. I yearned to know my purpose. Why was I put here? Surely it wasn't only to grow up, get married, add to the population, work, sleep, eat, repeat until I retired. After that I would fade into the oblivion that would eventually take me from this mortal plane. I wasn't buying it; not one iota of it. And I refused to succumb to the pious who insisted that the great scorekeeper was recording everything I did. At the end of my life I would face my creator and he would tell me the score. Nope, none of that for me.

I couldn't fathom this life was a game of sorts. You know what I mean. You play the game and someone keeps score. The person with the most points wins. There are multiple variations of this game. They're called religions. Some believe in virgins as the eternal reward. Others believe in fire and brimstone. Well it all feels like futility to me unless I leave a lasting and beneficial legacy behind.

So at age thirty I began to evaluate my life; when I wasn't jetting around the country to ply my trade at buying, improving and then selling businesses. At the end of the day, when I was alone with myself I would contemplate my accomplishments and regardless of how monumental they might appear to the people in my little slice of the world, they fell miserably short of filling a thimble as far as I was concerned.

The next twenty odd years would continue to push and prod me to find my path, my mission, my passion. That portion of my journey was mostly uphill. I struggled to fabricate fulfillment. I began with woodworking and became proficient at home remodeling. Then it was on to building businesses, negotiating deals, making money to afford bigger homes, luxury cars and other toys and trinkets that seemed to define success in the material world. These were all hollow victories.

Raising four children helped to ground me. But even that period was fleeting. Children grow up and move on leaving a long trail of memories behind. My children were no different. The most rewarding yet difficult part of child rearing is not having them around. Sure, we want them to be independent, to make a life, to leave the nest wings spread wide catching thermals that will enable them to soars higher than we did. Empty nests leave regret in their wake. What was once a full, hectic and frenetic world suddenly slowed. I began to run faster to try to keep my world spinning at the same speed. I didn't want to slow down. I didn't want to be alone with my thoughts. There were questions I kept locked away like some misshapen being that cried and pleaded for release.

When the house was empty, the beast would shake and rattle the doors of its cage. I fought the urge to release it; like some mythical beast that consumed everything in its path. The beast knew my name. It taunted me; it knew my secrets. The pull of its voice was intoxicating. I eventually succumbed to the need to embrace what I had kept locked away. Maybe its companionship would edify me or at least fill a portion of the yawning emptiness in my soul.

It wasn't until I began my gender transition in earnest that I discovered the purpose for my life. The beast had a name. At first I may have viewed gender dysphoria as a curse, a pox on my life, a complexity I wasn't equipped to manage without falling into an emotional abyss that threatened to blot my relevance and eviscerate my ability to influence anything in my world. Then I awoke one morning to an epiphany. Gender dysphoria wasn't a curse; it was a blessing. My condition was a gift. It opened my mind like scriptures opens the mind of the theologically inclined. A story unfolded, filled with realizations and revelations. Gender dysphoria wasn't an imaginary distraction. I was experiencing something unusual. As important, I wasn't alone. There was a community of people struggling with the same gender disassociation. No, I'm not delusional. Like every other revelation, knowledge is powerful and clarifying. Knowledge is an enabler. Beginning to understand gender dysphoria removed the shackles of stigma; helped me understand who I was and what

I was. I stopped questioning myself regarding these unconventional gender feelings.

I believe we're all imbued with strength of character enough to deal with whatever life throws in our path. Well, I firmly believe there is a purpose to my life and it includes living my authentic self. The woman inside has been yearning for voice, for expression. The voice wasn't that of a beast. The cries were merciful not threatening. She knew me. She is me. After all this time relief finally washed up on the shores of my life. But there was going to be a complication. In fact, there were going to be almost as many complications as there are grains of sand. The woman was ready to tear open the cocoon. Was I ready for her? Could I do this in a way that would enrich my life? I didn't want to do this if I was going to have to hide. I knew the rollout would be slow. I wanted it to be steady. I didn't want to be segregated from society. I felt the need to make a difference and she was telling me she would show me the way.

Some people in the community strive to blend in, to assimilate. That's their prerogative. They want comfort and safety. I'm with them up to a point. Maybe they're not cut out to be in the open, exposed and vulnerable. That's okay. Everyone is entitled to make their decisions and live with the consequences.

I consider myself a teacher, a leader and a mentor. I believe it's difficult to be all those things if you can't present an example grounded in reality. Writing a book is one thing. Living the book in the presence of others is the quintessential accomplishment. Unfortunately, being transparent, part of the crowd, one of the girls or the boys, along with the attendant cost, doesn't play well with the majority of the transgender community that doesn't have the financial resources to fund all of the surgeries that transform one gender to another. That's sad; but it's also reality and it's not a reality relegated to the transgender community. Jealously and unrest permeate society. The relatively small population in our community tends to magnify outliers.

I've always been the defender of the downtrodden, helper to the less fortunate. Maybe it's one of my personality flaws. I can't walk away from a fight. This fight is a life or death struggle for some. It's an opportunity to open the door of acceptance wider for younger generations to pass through without as much effort as my generation. There are detractors, haters, fear mongers; all of them bullies. I disdain bullies. Their prey didn't ask to be bullied and abused. Might does not always make right. I began to realize my voice could make a difference for others. I might be able to convert this journey, this struggle, this epiphany, into an elixir for society. The first threads of passion began to weave themselves together at around the half century mark.

Blending, assimilating and becoming another face in a crowd of faces so similar that I'd lose my relevance, was more than I was willing to accept. During my working years prior to transitioning, I was forced to evolve from an introverted person, pressed into service due to my profession, to market my firm's expertise. But I was never comfortable doing this. I believe it directly resulted from my discomfort behind the male façade. When I decided to transition, and two months prior to living full-time as my authentic female self, I started advocating for diversity, inclusion and unconditional equality.

All the trepidation I experienced from behind the male façade melted away when the rays of the sun shone brightly and warmly on my femininity. I took to speaking, training and advocating as if I was born for this. Wait; I *was* born for this!

"If we want an inclusive society, we need to include ourselves. That means we have to all be a part of ensuring that our country lives up to the ideals upon which it was founded." - Cyndi Lauper

"It takes a strong person to shrug off ignorance, bigotry and bias. Reacting to situations that are not ideal does a disservice to the reacting party (you) and empowers the other party who finds our existence inconsistent with their beliefs. Take a step back, gather yourself and collect your thoughts before responding. One of the best intellectual weapons in your arsenal is logic. When logic prevails, you carry the day. You may not have the luxury of winning over every person in every encounter but you will preserve dignity and self-worth by responding in an emotionally intelligent way. Life's not easy, regardless of our situation. But we can protect our feelings, our beliefs and ourselves by choosing our battles

wisely and learning from each encounter, no matter how potentially devastating it may feel." – Nikki DiCaro

Chapter 4

In the operating room the surgical team moved me from the travel gurney to the cold metal operating table. The move felt strange; as if I levitated from one table to the other. The operating table was narrow. My usual fear of falling strangely abandoned me. I wasn't troubled by the stage being set. I thought for a split second that maybe this part of my transition should be titled: Filet of Nikki. But before the thought blossomed into an excited utterance, the anesthesiologist administered the potion and the next thing I remember was awakening in recovery.

I can still feel the post-surgery wash of consciousness struggling for purchase. I was in a private room – nothing fancy but that was fine with me. Nurses checked the monitors, asked questions, read vital signs and smiled. Was this a dream? Was this whole segment of my life a dream? I tried to think back to what turned out to be four hours prior, when the whole episode threatened to change me physically. Was I really transformed? Was that body part I had been wishing to shrivel up and fall off really gone? Was I too harsh in my insistence upon a vagina and associated female portions of my anatomy?

I tried to focus. The lingering fog of anesthesia felt like it was playing tricks on me. Other than the medical professionals who floated in and out of my field of vision I felt nothing. I had watched videos of Vaginoplasty and the other components of male to female gender affirmation (bottom) surgery. As I watched each video, I felt phantom pain; as if I had been kicked in the groin and then had my genitals flayed. Nausea threatened to push me to disavow any desire for the surgery. It looked painful; almost sadistic. I could almost feel the howl of every severed nerve ending; the gaping hole between my legs crammed full of surgical packing begging to be closed up. How could anyone consider going through with this surgery after watching the graphic detail of the procedure. I laughed nervously at the thought of labeling the process "filet of penis". It took several months and the intervention of fate to get me past the battlements of trepidation and agree to have portions of my anatomy sliced and diced.

As I lay in the private hospital room; my penis gone, replaced by a neovagina, I tried to take inventory of my groin area. Telltale signs of male reproductive organ gone; check. Sensation in my legs and feet still there; check. Absence of anticipated agony; check. No pain, no screaming nerve endings. Maybe they didn't do the surgery. Maybe I was dreaming the entire episode. I didn't have sufficient command of my faculties to confirm my suspicions. It wasn't until the on-duty doctor made her rounds and inspected the bandaging that I knew something weird, wonderful and physically traumatic had occurred while I had voluntarily surrendered consciousness.

Three tubes protruded from the post-surgical dressing. The white dressing looked like combination panty briefs and chastity garment. It was wrapped securely around me. Memories of plaster casts on my leg and ankle after a bone break made me wonder how long before I started to itch. Two drainage tubes led to suction / collection balls. The third led to my Foley bag. This was more surreal than the video of the surgery. These three friends would accompany me for the next seven days of my recovery. I felt strange. I had tubes in my groin area; their ends were inside me doing whatever it is they were designed to do. There was no alarm; only a mild feeling of wonder trumped by a weird feeling of this being a dream. Maybe it was the residual effect of the drugs that had put me under.

Then there was the saline drip connected to the intravenous port on my right hand. The nurse showed me how the morphine drip worked. All I had to do was to push the little button and I'd receive instantaneous relief. Her smile was reassuring. My stomach churned at the thought of the anesthesia completely abandoning me, in its wake the pleading for pain relief. Hours passed as I lay prone in the hospital bed; my head elevated ten degrees. I always wondered what it would be like to lay around and have people wait on me. Even if they had served bon bons and high tea, the experience left me with an almost maddening desire to stand and walk around.

Food was delivered.; my first meal in forty-eight hours. Strangely (at this point there wasn't much that fell outside my personal Twilight Zone) I had little appetite. I tasted the Jell-O and drank water. I needed to hydrate since I hadn't drunk anything for thirty-six hours. I didn't feel queasy; that was a blessing. The green jiggly blob was almost tasteless but it was soothing to my throat. The nurse explained they had snaked a tube down my throat. She was right; there was a little rawness but again, nothing to write home about except when I tried to talk I sounded a little like Louie Armstrong.

The "every time I dozed off the nurse appeared" ritual began. Although I was connected to a pulse monitor, the shift nurse stopped by every two hours to check on me. What she didn't expect was that the Foley bag would need to be emptied every two hours. I had a penchant for water consumption and with each visit I requested more water, not food, just water. If nothing else, my lack of appetite would help me drop a few pounds during the hospital stay.

The first night I asked the nurse to forego the middle of the night interruption if I was asleep. The day before surgery bowel prep had me up most of the night and I wanted to try to reclaim some semblance of sleep pattern. I wasn't an insomniac but lately I was struggling to sleep through the night. Clearly, hospital routine was designed to convince me that going home as soon as possible was preferable to the twelve times a day poking and prodding.

My first full day of recovery brought boring television. You know, the box that hangs on the wall far away from the bed with the sound coming from the wired unit that controlled the channels. There wasn't much of interest to me. I thought about writing but my thoughts were still jumbled. And I hadn't brought my laptop to the hospital. I faded in and out of sleep between bouts of awakening appetite. Breakfast was bland but nourishing. I slowly ate the oatmeal with a touch of fruit, juice and hospital coffee. Thankfully my body didn't reject it. Maybe I really was there, awake and alive.

The first hint of pain summoned a call to the morphine button. The pain wasn't a bolt; more like a hello, I'm here and coming around. The morphine helped but it also worried me. The surgeon had prescribed an antibiotic and an opioid-laced pain killer to be used after I was discharged. I had heard about opioid-induced constipation. Thanks to the wonderful world of advertising! An acquaintance who had recently completed the same surgery complained about experiencing this problem. Another girl talked about the emotional upheaval she had experienced. I was acutely aware, maybe obsessed, with the worry of being irregular. I vowed not to allow my emotions to run roughshod over my newness.

I was feeling wonder and awe that four hours could grant my wish. I wanted to see my new body. For years, dating back to before puberty I would stand before a full-length mirror, my male betrayal tucked away as I stared at what I wanted my body to look like. I struggled to digest the fact that I finally accomplished what I desired for almost half a century. It was anti-climactic, at least while I was still snuggled uncomfortably in my post-surgical dressing with Matrix-like tubing protruding from me.

As day two approached and the specter of going home loomed large on the horizon I began to wonder what recovery would be. Recovery isn't defined by the time in the hospital. Recovery is defined by the events post-discharge. That's when I would be on my own and out of constant contact with medical professionals. I had booked a room at the post-surgery rest home (a/k/the recovery facility connected to the surgeon's offices). I had stayed there for the surgery prep that required drinking disgusting fluids, taking pills and my first every enema to encourage total evacuation while dining on clear liquids and chicken broth.

The departure date arrived. My first concern was being able to dress in street clothes and make the ride over uneven city streets without totally scrambling my brain and the area that was still raw from surgery. One short-term drawback to this type of surgery is the fact that you've got no choice but to sit on the affected area. We take the little things for granted. But this was no little thing. Every muscle seemed to connect to this area of my body. Every movement sent messages hurtling to my groin.

Thankfully there are various types of cushions (inflatable donuts) that can protect the area from direct contact with any surfaces. I made the mistake of waiting too long to purchase a quality unit. I settled for one that looked more like an inner tube than a shock absorbing cushion. That's what I got for not acting sooner. Regardless, the ride to the recovery facility was virtually pain free. Tom, the same Tom who delivered me for surgery, drove slowly and deliberately; swerving whenever conditions permitted in order to avoid pothole and rough road surface. My good friend who had recently undergone extensive hernia surgery volunteered to chauffeur me. He's a really good guy and a trooper. If he could soldier through his trauma, I could springboard off his resolve and make the trek to my temporary digs without complaining.

Arriving at the recovery facility we sat for a few moments. Our gazes locked and we smiled. "Two wounded warriors," Tom said turning smiles into laughter. We lugged my stuff to the portico and through the front door. I was a registered guest so I had a key. I didn't need to be buzzed in. Climbing the single flight of stairs we paused for a moment at the landing before making our way through the entry door and into my room.

Settling into the large room next to the bathroom, the room I occupied prior to surgery, I felt the first pangs of hunger. Tom sat for a moment to gather himself before departing. He was struggling to hide his discomfort. The hernia surgery had hit him hard. It was more extensive than he was led to believe.

After he left me alone I switched on the television for company. The sound of voices, regardless of their origin, was comforting. Being alone is overrated! I had prepared a few tasty morsels, nothing elaborate, and felt strong enough to shuffle from the bed to the small refrigerator to gather up a few items to jump start my reintroduction to eating. While in the hospital I was given antibiotics and medications to restart my excretory system. It never dawned on me that they could shut down my systems like that. Had I known, I wouldn't have had the fainting (it's still a bit sticky to use a non-masculine term to define a loss of consciousness) episode.

Surfing through the television channels while I was enjoying pickled hard boiled eggs (I learned that pickling eggs in the brine of store-bought capers gave them an invitingly salty taste) I found something that I could watch to pass the next days. I began to fear that eating might spark the need for a bowel movement. One of the surgeons I didn't select had warned about the potential for a fistula. It sounded like something you might see in a triple "X" rated movie. This set my surgery considerations back six months. The fear of a rupture between the bowel wall and the rear wall of the vagina and the potential for bowel resecting and a colostomy bag scared me enough to live with my unwanted genitalia for half a year longer than I wanted.

I made a point to enjoy things that would promote stool softening (exciting, I know) and I tempered my eating to allow my body to recover slowly. It was a blessing to be out of the hospital but I had to learn to deal with these tubes. Maintenance included emptying them as necessary throughout the day. I tucked them into the granny panties (female incontinence briefs) and they inevitably would tumble out and I'd have to corral them. By the end of the week's stay I'd be running for the examination table and its stirrups to get my short-term acquaintances banished to the medical waste bin.

Also, I had to sleep on my back, not my favorite position, until the tubing was removed. I was scared for my bodily functions to reengage. I'm not a big embracer of the unknown. And although male to female gender affirmation surgery is becoming more commonplace, there isn't an authoritative site that provides factual information on what to expect. This leaves the intrepid surgical candidate with anecdotal information from those choosing to document their exploits and feedback from friends who have gone before us to share their experiences.

One thing I learned from life is to take another's experiences with a boulder of sodium chloride. You can't evenly compare a person's experiences with what you can expect. It's a data point… only one data point. Individual experiences vary based upon each person's physiology, physical health, age, fitness, lifestyle, pain threshold, psychological health, resolve, endurance and overall outlook on life. This doesn't preclude surgical complications. They've been known to occur. The surgeon can't predict everything; and they are human and humans are prone to error. This thought unsettled me. What if my surgeon had a bad day? What if her investment portfolio had taken a dive; her personal life began to unravel, and so on and so forth?

It's best not to worry about things out of our control. And even if I believed what I was told and what I'd read, it was too late to put humpty penis back together again. Whatever the outcome, I was stuck with the result. I quickly became happy with the outcome and stayed astride the surgeon's instructions. Forcing myself to do things my body wasn't ready to undertake would exacerbate whatever upheaval my body had already undergone. I regularly reminded myself this surgery was not natural. Although nature played a trick on me by not matching my external with my internal, I could not will my body to do things it wasn't prepared to do.

Patience became my unwelcome friend. Being master or mistress of my universe became a drug, an intoxicant. I monitored my body. The pain level was probably a 2 on a scale of 1 – 10. Although I kept the oxycodone pill vial within reach, I had no desire to pop one; the fear of constipation and worse, addiction, probably helped to keep the pain in check. I've heard some pain is psychosomatic. I wasn't going to freak myself into a problem. I wasn't going to allow someone else's negative experiences to drive me. When pain surfaced, I took an NSAID. I also drank water and carbonated seltzer until I imagined my organs would float away. If I was billed for the number of times that Foley was emptied, I would have run up a huge tab!

On day five of my post-hospital recovery, the physician assistant and the nurse from the surgeon's office informed that I'd be having the tubes removed on day six. They had visited daily to check my progress. The ladies were complimentary and uplifting. I knew some of it was designed to boost my emotions and support my recovery. Hearing positive things always helps to increase morale. On hospital discharge day, the attending physician removed the bandaging. Since then I had been wearing feminine incontinence briefs; changing at least once daily due to the levels of drainage.

The thought of discharge made me wary of my ability to make the transition from under the watchful eye of the professionals to my little imperfect world of life. I was excited and worried. Dilation, a six-month process, would begin on the day the tubes were removed – The Matrix Unplugged. The thought of inserting hard objects into my vagina to maintain its depth and caliper made me shudder. I know, the vagina is a female intake point for male exhaust. But that wasn't why I decided to complete the physical correction. Sex was an afterthought. So far after all the other thoughts it resided in a different area code. I desired my external to reflect my internal. I didn't want to be betrayed by my plumbing. Again, with no reference point regarding how much pain was "normal" at

27

this point in the recovery process, I had no idea what to expect when dilation became my newest friend.

The first of many weird, and I'd like to think wonderful, things that took a while to adjust to was opening my legs for a vaginal inspection. If anything about this experience was going to be surreal, this was right up there with all the other first time events!

I was beginning to imagine life without my manmade temporary appendages. The thought of a shower after eight long days of recovery made me smile. If I had to have the tubes out and the dilators in… and out… in order to enabling showering, I was all in! I had washed my hair in the sink three times and sponged my body during those early days of recovery, but there's nothing like the feel of warm water washing over me as I savor every moment of cleaning. Of all the time between surgery and going home, shower time was rapidly becoming the prize, the brass ring, the winning bingo number.

I wandered down to the first floor of the building and into the lobby of the doctor's office. I was wearing a night shirt that broke at the knee and thigh high woolen socks; the hook of the Foley bag over my right index finger. The drainage tubes and suction balls were tucked conspicuously into a clean incontinence brief. I looked mildly pregnant. That was another of those strangely welcome thoughts. More uncertainty breached my psychological ramparts. These things were going to be removed and I would be able to wear street clothes. Four feet of surgical packing would also be extracted and I'd receive my personal dilation devices along with instructions. Fear leached into my heart and I felt suddenly chilled. Every new experience brought a combination of wonder, expectation and dread in equal parts.

The receptionist warmly welcomed me. This team knew how to help people feel comfortable. I was invited into an examination room without waiting. Just when I thought things were strange, they just got stranger. The reclining examination chair/table had stirrups up and a small metal table holding a vaginal spreader and a few other feminine examination items. I remember hearing about gynecologic examinations from women who had made stops in my life on the way to wherever they were headed. I was going to experience what they talked about.

Placing my bare feet in the stirrups I imagined things that had no place in the doctor's office. I felt a tingle of sensuality as I sat in a vulnerable position.

When the nurse and physician assistant entered, I smiled. They were going to liberate me, unshackle me, and I wasn't going to allow my fear of the unknown to ruin the moment. As they checked the affected area, more words of encouragement.

The first to be removed were the drainage tubes; one on either side of my vagina near the top of the opening. I can still remember watching. At the end of the tube a rectangular intake value popped out with the sound of something large passing quickly through a small opening. I think I squelched! They applied small bandages to each incision. Next came the catheter. "This one might sting," the nurse said. I gritted my teeth for the procedure. There was nothing to grab; no tongue depressor to bite down upon. The feeling of release was strange. The tug of the plastic hose and the resistance from my shortened urethra made me wince. When the tubes were out I think a phrase from Dr. Martin Luther King scrolled across my mind's eye.

All the while my feet were firmly planted in the stirrups and my body almost prone on the cushioned and reclined examination table. The thought of being in a place my birth gender assured I would never experience firsthand, stopped pulling at me as unnatural. Everything I had experienced and would be experiencing threatened to be nouveau, fascinating, and maybe a touch too close to unexpected. Surprisingly, none of this bothered me, not even the unconditional surrendering of genitalia that had contributed to the birth of four children. The appendage I sometimes enjoyed for the hormones it generated to facilitate muscle development, abhorred for promoting hair loss and made wearing tight female clothes difficult and nearly impossible without the aid of very snug and very uncomfortable undergarments. I had wished it away on more occasions than I can remember beginning around age ten. It may have been much earlier but more than fifty years of memories and experiences seem to have crowded out the very early recollections.

"We're going to remove the packing. You're doing great!" The physician assistant said. Both ladies continued to bolster my ego. I'm sure

29

I was as fragile as centuries old porcelain although I didn't feel it. Maybe I was still numb. I'd heard for every hour of anesthesia the body requires one month to fully evacuate it. I had been under for almost four hours and I had been post-anesthesia for a week. Maybe I wasn't firing on all cylinders.

She began to pull the packing; the long ribbon extracted slowly and deliberately. The pressure between my legs lessened slightly with each foot of material. It almost felt like she was unwinding a spool of string and pulling it through an opening that created slight resistance.

When the last inches exited, I breathed again. I didn't realize I had been holding my breath. I never understood why we unconsciously hold our breath when we anticipate a new experience. The PA smiled. I returned the gesture. Relief came in waves. I was free! I could begin to resume a normal lifestyle. But what *is* normal? The moment of truth was about to unfold. "Was I ready?" I asked myself. Everything was out. She was going to show me how to put something in. I was going to redefine normal yet again.

"Now we're going to show you how to dilate." She lifted a pale purple cloth pouch with four narrow compartments, a cover flap and single binding string. "These are your dilators. There are three of them. They are purple, blue and green. We need you to dilate for twenty minutes, four times a day for the first month, three times a day for two months and then two times a day for three months. After that you should dilate once a day. Sexual intercourse can count as one dilation. But no sex for at least the first three months. You have to give yourself time to heal. That normally only takes three months." She rattled off the instructions without missing a beat. Clearly, she was a veteran of many unshackling sessions. She emphasized the 'no sex' imperative as if I was going to run out and grab the first John I saw.

I shook off the thought of intercourse and who might want to be impaled before they were completely healed. My sex drive had an out of service transmission. I assured her I would be compliant. She showed each of the dilators; three cylinders (thick, thicker and thickest) rounded at the business end and flat at the other with a subtle upward bend in the initial 20% of the rounded end. The upward bent section was slightly narrower than the area with the dots. There were five evenly spaced while dots along the top of each to indicate depth. There were no cords or battery compartments. "You're probably not going to need the purple one. We'll start with the blue one." The attending nurse opened a tube of lubricant, applied a liberal bead to the first third of the cylinder and then spread it with her finger. The PA inserted the dilator. I felt almost nothing. The surgical area was still numb. The nerve endings were recovering from the shock and trauma inflicted upon them.

"It's that easy. Let try the green one," she said as if we were going to sample tea or a dessert. Repeating the lubrication step she inserted the green one with almost no resistance from my body.

"You're not going to have any problem dilating," the physician assistant said confidently. I began tallying the number of dilation events times twenty minutes each I would be undertaking during the next six months.

"You're also going to douche once a week for eight weeks. Then you can douche one or twice a month after that." She held up a box with two douching bottles and two packets of povidone iodine. "You'll want to use the medicated douche." Another surreal moment flashed across my mind's eye. The term "douche" is French for "a spray or shower of water". According to the dictionary it is also the term for "an obnoxious or contemptible person." I tamped down the desire to giggle. Using the term "douche" as a verb rather than an adjective tickled a sad and adolescent memory.

"Okay, you're all good and you'll probably be going home tomorrow," the PA said with a flourish. I wasn't expecting to be discharged two days early. Warning bells sounded in the distance. I was going to be alone and an hour away from the doctor sooner than I expected. I never thought I'd experience severing the umbilical cord again; not in my middle years anyway. I shook off the thought and smiled. I guess I was progressing nicely. Following pre-surgery and post-surgery instructions to the letter seemed to be paying off.

"You can shower but don't wash the area." She didn't have to define "the area". "Stand with your back to the water and let it wash over you. Don't' use a handheld showerhead to rinse the area. Don't use any soap on the area directly," she continued with the don'ts and don'ts of post-surgical care. I was excited to be free to stand under warm water and wash. I had almost forgotten how good a shower could feel. I needed to shower; as if it was essential to my well-being.

Gathering myself I climbed down from the examination chair, dressed and padded through the reception area and slowly up one flight of stairs to my room. I prepared for the shower; almost as if the ritual was sacred and solemn. I savored every step. Even the odiferous artifacts of bowel cleansing in the community bathroom by one of the soon to be newest members of the "girls' club" didn't dampen my joy.

I ran the shower to warm the bathroom. We were cresting the first third of December and the days were typically cold and dreary. The recovery facility was an old converted three-story house and was probably the home of a prominent citizen during its early years of existence. Its high ceilings and large windows were stately but they weren't conducive to warm rooms. Stepping into the shower was slow and deliberate. Part of me was concerned about getting the surgery area wet. But when the first droplets of water kissed my flesh all worry washed away in the stream of inviting, clean and warm water.

I savored that shower like none I could remember. The simple pleasures, taken for granted, become essential to survival in our civilized and domesticated world. I leaned back to allow water to flow across my body and down through the newly minted vaginal area. Staring at the construction zone I tried to process how the area looked before alterations. I wasn't amazed not awe-struck. I was comfortable with the change. I felt like another layer of aging and unwelcome façade had been stripped away.

Toweling off I tried to block the thread of concern that tugged at the seam of my consciousness. I'd have to pack and lug and take the hour ride home. My good friend Tom was going to come by to chauffeur me yet again. The man was a godsend. He is another example of how the universe works when you're open to the messages.

I met Tom serendipitously three years prior. I had this desire to join a mixed bowling league. At the time, I was living ten minutes from nearby lanes and decided on a whim to sign up expecting to be recruited for summer league. A week after I submitted my application I received a call asking if I was interested in joining a team mid-year as they had lost a bowler. I took the plunge and appeared the following week. Two weeks later I overheard a conversation between one of my teammates and this well-spoken and confident man about a new business venture. Over the ensuring week I mulled the conversation. The next bowling night I casually approached Tom. His team happened to be bowling on an adjoining lane.

He was gracious and open and I think a bit intrigued by my background and experience with business formation, start up and operations. He agreed to share his business plan with me and after I sliced and diced it and returned the extensively marked up work I figured he'd dismiss me as a crank, a charlatan or some other unsavory societal aberration. His reaction couldn't have been more opposite my expectations. My edits garnered fast respect from the entrepreneur and our friendship developed quickly.

More than a year later I invited him to dinner at a local pub to reveal my authentic self. I was moved to tears by his unexpectedly open and welcoming response. He rose, a smile broadly displayed across his face. As he walked over to my chair he opened his arms and welcomed me with a big hug which he held for a long time. I fought back tears as I thanked him for being gracious and understanding.

"Why are you thanking me? I should be thanking you for trusting me with your secret!" He released me, smiled again and returned to his seat across the table from me. "I don't think you understand how honored I am that you shared this with me." Somehow my revelation strengthened his respect and admiration for me. In a method only Tom could employ, he contemplated and evaluated and offered his sincerest thoughts about my revelation. "I had no idea, if that matters to you. How long have you felt this way and when did you realize you were transgender?" He pronounced 'transgender' solemnly and with clear diction.

"I've known for most of my life; about fifty years," I answered almost apologetically.

"Wow! I can't imagine how you kept this in for so long," he said earnestly.

Tom became yet another example of living your life honestly and with a healthy respect and engagement of others for who they are, without drama, judgment or prejudice garners respect. Revealing something deeply personal about yourself will land gently upon the heart of the people who have appreciated your friendship. The ability to articulate a revelation and to trust your heart that you're doing the right thing, enriches the experiences of life and invites true friends to celebrate with you.

Tom arrived at the recovery facility on time; you could set your clock by his punctuality. We were walking wounded. Both of us were limited to lifting no more than ten pounds. As I was packing for my departure I fretted over how much 'stuff' I was bringing home and how I so badly miscalculated the need.

Navigating my excessive and overweight baggage to the first floor and into his car we stood for a moment to recover from the obvious strain. Another reality of the surgery crept upon me. I wasn't accustomed to physical limitations. I had been a body builder; muscular, toned and fearless. Things had dramatically changed and I was going to have to accept that my strength was never going to approximate those salad days.

Settling gingerly in the passenger seat onto the inner tube for the second time; Tom engaged in conversation the entire ride. The man's compassion, he knew that talking would deflect from my discomfort and his as well, may be equaled but it is not surpassed by any other friends of the same caliber. I was playing the unaccustomed role of passenger; ceding control to a man. I had to remind myself I wasn't that gender any longer. If there was any doubt, all I had to do was pull back the waistband of my panties to confirm.

The sixty-minute ride passed quickly. Tom was gracious with his conversation. Our discussions swung from business to personal and back again without breaking literary stride. Parking in front of my townhome in Yardley, Pennsylvania I felt relief that we had arrived and I wasn't feeling raw or pained by the excursion. We sat for a moment, both relieved as we prepared to alight and transfer my belongings from the trunk of the car, up several steps and into the house. Working my way out of the car, still feeling foreign in maxi-skirt, sweater and slip on flats, I stood on wobbly legs. We walked slowly and deliberately taking one step at a time. Was I receiving a free preview of old age? Another thread of dread attempted to weave itself into my psyche.

We made the climb up the seven concrete steps and I wasn't any worse for it. Discomfort was palpable but not overwhelming. Lying around for a couple of weeks at the front end of recovery did nothing to improve my muscle tone. I felt lazy and out of shape. I was a long way from the days when exercise was an obsession. Muscle building to maintain a beach body was one of the palliatives to deflect my feminine calling. Obviously, it didn't work. Most palliatives are only temporary. For me, muscle building was a placebo.

I was a pretty serious fitness freak. This sedentary lifestyle was causing my mature body to betray signs of slacking off; threatening to add another dragline to my psyche. Funny how aging makes you work harder to achieve what came easily when we were younger. The only thing that seemed to come more easily was the willingness to ease the foot off the accelerator. I was going to force myself to take it easy and enjoy the recovery.

I knew I wasn't ready for the recliner or a stair lift. I craved a comfortable chair or a bed like a pregnant woman craves her favorite food. Slipping off my flats I eased onto the sofa. The comfortable chair welcomed me. With my feet propped on the sofa cushion I wiggled me toes. There was comfort in going barefoot, aside from the typical girl thing. I enjoyed the moment. They came often.

Tom slid onto one of the two side chairs looking haggard; signs of a painful recovery painted on his features in stark contrast to his usual positive demeanor. We were both wiped out. "Who ordered this to happen?" I asked. We both laughed, shrugging off the question. The realization that recovery would be slow and plodding wasn't lost on either of us. Regardless of how vibrant we felt and how fertile our minds, the body tended to be the coward, the wilting lily; retreating under the constant pressure of time.

I began to think about how I might have prepared more aggressively for the surgery. Another of my character flaws. Maybe I could have exercised more; adjusted my diet to drop a couple of unwanted pounds. The holy grail of improvement haunted me like a persistent and restless spirit. This was yet another mental grilling that would serve no useful purpose. Dismissing the thought, I smiled. Tom's gaze caught mine and we laughed together as he broke the ice with one of his patented "master of the obvious" statements. We chatted about life; the inevitability of age and the fact that youth was wasted on the young.

Fifteen minutes later Tom rose slowly. I watched from my prone position on the sofa. I wanted, no I needed to stand. That's what a good hostess does. Gathering myself I pushed up and off. My legs felt a little surer under me. We enjoyed a glass of cold water. Funny how the simple things come to feel like a luxury after a physical or emotional trial.

We embraced. Since my transition, hugging everyone seemed to come naturally. Prior to revealing my authentic self, very rarely did I hug anyone except family members and even that felt awkward. Yes, I know, Italians and Sicilians are supposed to hug and plant a kiss on the cheek. La Cosa Nostra tradition was plastered all over the cinema! But this was different.

I hugged newly minted acquaintances; men and women. I thought about that phenomenon. I may have caught them off guard and caused discomfort. That wasn't my objective. I wanted them to feel the person, the human being, the 'someone' just like them. I was never denied a hug. Some were warmer and more natural than others. One thing is certain, the hug when we parted company was warm and welcoming. It conveyed a message of understanding and acceptance. Was it the newness of my life or was it the spectacle of a transwoman. No wait, that's not right if you believe the vocal minority who have declared war on transgender; nobody wants to admit our existence. Forget the people who can't fathom anyone outside their narrow boundaries. They have to be 'them' their entire life!

There was definitely sincerity and genuineness in people's reactions, regardless of the vocal minority's objections. Hugging was the salve, the unspoken apology, the welcoming acceptance that said everything was okay without a word being spoken. Friendly and accepting people were the apologists for the Neanderthals who insisted on hurling hateful and destructive words and actions towards those who didn't fit their narrow-minded view of life.

Alone with my thoughts I conjured up reflection. I've been circumspect since I sat alone awaiting the call to the operating room. Turning my lens inward has been a common practice throughout my life. No matter the depth and breadth of those mental deep dives, I always emerged with a lingering question; who am I. It wasn't until I lay in the staging area at the hospital that clarity washed over me like the cleansing water of renewal. Two years prior I had resolved to make a difference, leave a mark, change the world. I finally knew my calling. But did I? Did I really grasp the enormity of the task? The gender change enabled me to channel energy previously lost every time I passed through the gender divide. The barrier, the force field separating my birth façade from my authentic self, extracted an emotional toll every time I made the crossing.

Towards the end of the duality period – at least three months prior to January 2016 – I agonized over going back; stepping behind the male facade. Stripping off all outward signs of femininity brought tears and anxiety. I waited until the last minute before bed on Sunday evening to remove the last vestiges of my authentic self. Press on nails, the easy way to a temporary salon-look manicure, were the last casualties. Reverting to the façade of my birth gender became impossible to bear. I could no longer swing easily between them.

Until the moment I was wheeled into surgery I could have called time out. I could have walked away and forestalled all the recovery, the anticipated pain and prolonged healing process. I could have eliminated the unknown by maintaining my membership in the transgender pre-op club. There is a condescending phrase unkind people use to describe such club. I'll leave that to your imagination. If you know that phrase, think about it and how destructive it is. Lose it as you would want others to lose any pejoratives that could be used to describe you.

Changing the public view of me was one thing. Changing the physiology was another. This permanent; no restart button, no "do over", no biological eraser. If I completed this transformation I would trade my membership card in one club for the coveted membership card in another. This gender change was many things to me. The biological conformity to a female fulfilled a hope and dream since adolescence. I didn't want to be reminded of the error in my façade. The biological building inspector who should have caught the errant hormonal infiltration during gestation was either absent or ignored the human engineering plans from which I was designed.

I didn't step away from the gurney. I didn't go home, go directly home without passing surgery and without collecting my female genitalia. I couldn't. Not because I prepaid for the right of passage – an expensive toll booth because insurance companies have failed to support the cost of such surgery. Not because I might embarrass myself by changing my mind. No, I stayed the course; defended the decision because I would have regretted withdrawing what I had worked so hard to achieve. Fifty years of waiting assured me this was the right decision. Whatever the outcome, I would have my female anatomy; even if it was accompanied by pain, post-surgery maintenance and other physiological changes driven by major hormonal shifts.

This lasting, irreversible alteration, although fraught with risks, gave me the ability to talk the talk and walk the walk about being a transwoman in living color. I was committed to being my authentic self and I was becoming a bit of a minor celebrity with speaking engagements, coaching and consulting opportunities. In order for me to speak of the entire transition process I needed firsthand experience. There were too many pretenders. Too many people who dabbled in gender transition. Many self-proclaimed authorities who preached "do as I say" without adding "not as I do". I could not face myself if I was disingenuous. I couldn't teach, coach or counsel if I couldn't look my audience in the eye and speak from the depths of my soul.

Authenticity means many things to many people. And my definition doesn't necessarily translate into the definition by which others live. That's fine. Personal choice is (or should be) alive and well. My decision to go all the way was grounded in the need to fix what nature chose to screw up. After surgery, I would be equipped with an almost complete set of experiential tools in my consultant's handbag.

I reminded myself this was my decision. Nobody forced me into this. I had completed over two hundred hours of electrolysis. If I could endure four consecutive hours per week of facial deforestation, I could deal with full recovery from fairly serious surgery that delivered what had been a dream for almost my entire life.

Chapter 5

Tom's departure left me alone in my recently occupied surroundings. I had moved a month ago from a town ten miles north in order to be closer to Philadelphia for my commute to work. Being alone can be cathartic or it can be nerve wracking. 'Alone' never really left me to myself. Or maybe 'alone' ushered in the thought goblins.

Here's your chance to drill into the girl's brain and plant that seed of doubt. Seed already planted? Well get in there and till the soil and add fertilizer to enable to doubt to blossom into misgivings and loss of confidence.

Shuffling around the first floor of the townhome I felt pressure in my loins. The doctor advised to rest as much as possible and to give healing a long runway (my words not hers). I was never good at sitting still. I've been accused of having ants in my pants. I should have inquired the type of ants to which they were referring.

Several minutes later I decided to make my way upstairs to the master bedroom and to begin the task of dilating twenty minutes, four times daily for the first month of recovery. Grabbing one of three travel bags I climbed the stairs. I don't think stair climbs ever felt like a mountain; at least not until today. We don't realize how lucky we are to have unfettered mobility until that mobility is compromised.

I was worried. Another new experience. Regardless of whether the dilation trial run was successful, this was the real thing; on my time and without the underpinning of the medical staff within reach. At the top of the stairs I stopped to allow my body to catch up. Turning right I crossed the threshold into the bedroom. The bed lay empty, the promise of comfort beckoning. Pulling back the fluffy white comforter, blanket and top sheet I positioned pillows against the padded headboard to support my back. Laying out the incontinence sheet (plastic on the bottom, absorbent materials on the business side) I stared at it as if there was an answer to a yet-to-be formulated question. Taking a roll of paper towels, I tore off four sheets and laid them next to the black bag with the white handles. This little designer gift bag held the dilators, mirror and lubricating gel.

Climbing into bed I didn't realize how high above the floor the mattress sat. "Is this how my mother, all of five-foot tall, felt when she was faced with getting herself into bed?" Sliding onto the bed I shimmied my bottom until I was centered over the protective covering. Everything between my navel and the upper third of my thighs was still numb from surgery. It would be weeks before swelling subsided and feeling returned.

As I lubricated the blue dilator I examined the results of surgery. It looked raw and angry. But for all the upheaval, there was no pain. I stared at the area and wondered how such a complex procedure could be accomplished in less than four hours. I also tried to recall what it felt like to have a male appendage. My memory seemed to have deleted that part. Maybe it was the anesthesia. It didn't matter. Not at this juncture. I was thrilled to have come through without writhing pain and monumental discomfort.

With the dilator inserted I started the timer on my phone. I considered what I thought this would feel like and compared it to the act of intercourse. This was another foreign thought process. I wasn't sold, convinced or persuaded that there'd ever be anything other than an inanimate object probing my Lexi. There seemed to be this thing among women to give their Va JJ a "G" rated name. I've heard "Suzie" used the describe the vagina, I decided I'd call mine "Lexi" to eliminate any confusion with a friend named Suzie.

The first at home dilation was uneventful although I stared at the timer on the phone wishing it would move faster. I began to realize that twenty minutes could seem like an eternity.

The process was sloppy but not painful. Maybe it was because everything in the vicinity was numb. The marvelous part of the outcome was the lack of pain. I thought about the Oxycodone the doctor has prescribed – thirty days' worth. My pain, if you can call what I was feeling 'pain', was probably a 2 on a Likert scale that topped out at 10. No desire to take Oxy. I feared addiction but feared constipation more. The looming potential for a fistula would be compounded by irregularity. No amount of pain relief was worth risking a perforation into the vaginal canal.

Dilation – four times a day four hours apart for the first month – was going to dominate my world until the end of three months; at which time dilation stepped down from four times to three times then reduced to twice a day. I needed to make peace with the process. Every decision carries consequences.

Can't do the consequences, don't do the decision!

Dilation provided more reflection time. My life was becoming one huge self-therapy session. The first few days at home I tried to focus on writing. I was experiencing writer's block. That scared me more than the surgery and recovery. I had been writing continuously for eleven years. I worried that the creativity, drive and determination to write had abandoned me as quickly as it had seized me. Maybe it was the anesthesia.

We tend to blame most bad outcomes on uncontrollable forces. In my case, maybe it was warranted. Maybe writer's block was the direct result of worry. I inherited worry as one of the ancestral values that was passed from generation to generation. Some value. When worry gets in the way of progress, it quickly loses its value.

My mind summoned the surgical decision file from the folder at the front of my mental file cabinet. I considered how this part of my transition had transpired. I guess I wasn't finished analyzing and reanalyzing how I got here. Part of this persistent analysis was designed to prepare me to answer questions and speak intelligently to any audience that requested my presence.

I had consulted another surgeon several months prior to making my selection and going through with my decision. She was post-op transgender and an accomplished surgeon. She had given me so much information, most of it negative, that I left her office doubting I'd go through with any surgery related to changing my physical appearance. This was one of the most significant setbacks in my life. I had psyched myself up for the consultation; ginned up a number of questions and dismissed the steep consult fee. *I was doing this.* Everything I read about this surgeon told me she was qualified and experienced. I'm not sure where and when the wheels fell off the decision cart. Maybe it was the specter of negative outcomes. Maybe it was her warning that every one of her surgical patients had gained significant weight during the recovery year. Maybe it was her demeanor.

This surgeon spent a significant portion of the interview convincing me I didn't want to go through with this. Maybe her planting the seeds of doubt was her way of vetting candidates to determine if they were emotionally capable of handling the changes. She had dented my resolve. I needed to retool, bang out the dents and evaluate the risks against the rewards. Time for a time out.

Months later during one of my regular weekly calls with a heart friend, we discussed surgeons' qualifications. If you're suffering gender dysphoria and struggling with transition, there are many topics around transition that will infiltrate your conversations with others like you. My heart friend had done deeper research than I had regarding one of the local surgeons. Our discussion heated to a slow boil as she allayed my fears and countered each of my arguments against this surgeon. After the call, I reconsidered my options. I still wasn't certain I would make the effort to discuss bottom surgery with another surgeon. And if I did entertain these discussions, there would be no commitment to surgery during such consultation.

My third surgical consultation occurred on a whim. Well, maybe not so cavalierly. It was a slow day at the office. I decided to call the third surgeon and schedule a consult. I had been reviewing her website and searching the web for reviews and feedback. Her credentials were solid and impressive. When I get an idea, I usually run it down, research it and run it through the mental wash, rinse and spin cycle several times. You might consider this an obsession or a compulsiveness. I wouldn't argue that conclusion.

I placed the call and an appointment was scheduled. As the appointment approached I wasn't nervous. Arriving at the office I felt comfortable, settled, grounded. The office was clean, professional and felt a little like coming home. The trepidation and anxiety from prior consultations faded away. I wasn't going to the appointment to make a decision. Maybe that's why I wasn't nervous. I was greeted warmly by the receptionist, my information taken. After being led to one of the clean and tidy examination rooms I sat alone and ran through my questions.

After a short waiting period the consultation began. The surgeon offered to waive the initial consultation fee if I had attended the Keystone Conference. The Keystone Conference in an annual LGBTQ four-day event that takes place in and around Harrisburg, Pennsylvania.

Waiving the fee was a welcome relief. Something felt right about her. The consult was also attended by her physician assistant. This was different from the other consults – a second attendee (sound practice to protect against potential lawsuits). The surgeon launched into her sales pitch. It was polished and thorough. She asked about the WPATH requirements and where I was with them. By the end of the consult it was time to know how far out her waiting list.

I don't know why I felt compelled to know the waiting list. I had convinced myself this was not going to be an immediate decision. But something had changed. We clicked; or the universe was signaling this was the right surgeon for me.

"How far out is the wait list?" I asked. The surgeon looked to her assistant.

"We're out to April... no May," the PA replied.

"May huh. You're really busy," I said.

"We perform two surgeries a day two days a week." I quickly calculated sixteen surgeries a month. I thought that felt like a healthy stream of medical practice. She had been performing surgeries of this type for ten years. She had performed several hundred surgeries; a significant number for what was purported to be a tiny community in relation to the general population. We talked about complications, recovery period, post-surgical maintenance, what to expect in terms of look and feel of the vaginal area.

"You'll be able to have intercourse three months after surgery if your recovery is normal. And you should have all the feelings, including orgasms, as a woman." The surgeon smiled as she provided assurances. These points were important to a number of transwomen. They really didn't strike a chord with me. I wasn't in this for the sexual. I hadn't given much thought to intercourse and orgasms. Maybe it was the muting of my male sex drive by eighteen months of testosterone blockers and estrogen hormone therapy.

"Do you normally have cancellations?" I asked.

"Sometimes people cancel or reschedule but it doesn't happen often," the surgeon said confidently.

"If I get on you waiting list now, can you let me know if you have any cancellations? If you do, can you move me up on the list?" I couldn't believe I was pressing for a surgery date. All the confidence of this being a casual encounter flew away as if suffering from a chronic case of flight bias.

"I don't know how my schedule looks. Can you check my calendar?" She turned and asked her PA.

"I'll grab your calendar," the PA said. She disappeared for a few minutes.

She returned moments later with the schedule. "We have an opening on December 7."

"That's three and a half weeks away. Can I have that date?" I asked as if I had come to the dealership to buy the car regardless of the price.

"That might not be enough time to get all your paperwork in order. We follow WPATH guidelines. You'll need a physical, EKG, blood work and two therapist letters. And if you want insurance to consider covering this, you may not have enough time for them to process your claims."

"The money's not a problem. I'm planning to fund this up front and apply for reimbursement." More commitment as if an external force was pulling the strings and pushing the buttons. "And the other things I can get done. Mazzoni is my doctor. I already have one letter. I can easily get a second." As I spoke I realized this visit wasn't a lark. This was preplanned and I was being guided. Things fell into place; tumblers in a complex combination lock being expertly manipulated.

"We can put you on the list for December 7!" The PA said. "We'll give you a full set of instructions and several prescriptions." The doctor smiled as she listened to the interchange.

The surgeon interjected, "You're going to do well. I feel your confidence. You know what you want and you are confident. That's the most important thing. If I thought you weren't ready, we'd ask you to take more time to think it over. But I feel like you're ready." She had touched every button, flipped every switch. She read me better than I imagined. I guess when you do something long enough your intuition serves to evaluate verbal and non-verbal responses to support a conclusion.

Suddenly the impossible felt possible. Trepidation that had been lurking, waiting for an opportunity to pounce was vanquished by this sudden chance to make a decision. The stars aligned. I felt power coursing through me. Any clouds of doubt surrendered to the blazing sun of possibility.

I made the down payment for surgery and received five prescriptions to fill, along with several pages of instructions. There was much to do and the time between surgical consult and surgery date was compressed. There were foods I should consider, foods, herbs, supplements, prescription and over-the-counter medications I should avoid. The biggest adjustment was refraining from hormone therapy and the potential impact including facial hair growth, muscle development, etc. That concerned me more than the surgery. As an afterthought, one benefit of surgery was removal of testicles and testosterone production. I wasn't going to need Spironolactone any longer. That was great news for my liver.

Looking over the long list of requirements, I wasn't worried. I had managed more complex requirements in shorter time windows. This was destiny or kismet or preordained; pick your word or phrase. My life found clear direction when I opened myself to the universe. That may sound contrived. Don't knock it until you try it!

I was excited; the joy of possibility, achieving another goal, passing another milepost. My life was moving in the right direction at a good clip. When I arrived home I called friends to tell them about my surgery. They congratulated me, after brief pauses. They were processing the speed of my transition. I guess I was full of surprises; this being the biggest to date. I had taken my authentic self like a cyclone; moving rapidly and devouring every obstacle in my path. I think my approach of educating myself quickly, spring boarding off the knowledge I gained from my friends and making decisions with less than 100% of the facts, was a bit disarming. The rapid process and decision-making was a learned trait from many years under the tutelage of three very accomplished professional mentors. Their training drifted easily into my personal life.

When I received congratulatory responses from my sisters (trans and cis) I cried tears of joy. There's little better in life than the support of exceptional friends. Yes, I repeated this statement. It's worth committing to memory and using as a yardstick against which to measure progress in your life. These people had been the bedrock of support. Their unconditional love and support helped me break down the male façade and cart the pieces to the emotional landfill. Our relationships were synergistic and symbiotic. We supported each other at the greatest inflection points in our lives. When one of us broke a barrier, we shared the experience with the others. This instilled confidence and provided a knowledgeable reference point for any of us who were facing the same or similar barrier. It also gave us a resource, a shoulder upon which to lean if there were complications. Most importantly, my friends provided a sympathetic ear and honest feedback delivered in a loving and caring way.

The timing of the open surgery slot wasn't dumb luck. Things in my life didn't occur without purpose. My job was to ensure I was open to all of these occurrences, messages, etc. December 7 was strategic. It wasn't going to be an infamous date in my life. Early December, on the advent of the Christmas Holidays, provided the perfect backdrop to extended leave. Things at the office were usually slow beginning after December 10. I had a large bank of unused vacation time I would lose if not used before the end of the calendar year. I had also accumulated a significant block of extended leave time I could use during my convalescence. This provided an opportunity to recover without taking a month of days away from work. To ease the time away from the office, I was set up to work remotely until the doctor released me to return to active duty.

The weight of my decision finally reached me when I lay in bed trying to read one of the three books I had been perusing. As with any major decision, and this was one of the biggest and the most irreversible of my life, I ran through the process of reaching this point. Was I sure? Did I really mean to schedule surgery to take away what's been a defining thing for me? I began to think about all the relationships, the intimacy, the child

47

births. It's funny how the mind works; churning up all of the silt that had settled at the mouth of the river of my life. The channel to the open waters of gender expression and my authenticity was shallow. I guess I needed to dredge the channel in order to allow the draft of this decision to safely make open water.

After settling myself emotionally I reconciled the decision and the yearning. "You're already there, DiCaro. You're already living your true gender, your authentic self – at least the public view." That last phrase "at least the public view" felt like an indictment. Some days when walking from the train to the office I felt liberated; but not completely. There was still a part of me anchored to the past; to my birth gender. I pondered whether I was a fraud, an imposter in women's clothing. Segments of the world felt that way about me and my trans-sisters. I didn't want to betray who I was because of uncertainty. I began to wish I had been born in the correct body. Wishing wasn't going to change that. History proved wishing is relegated to wells and stars.

"If you really and truly want this so badly, you'll stop beating yourself up," the voice of hope piped up. She understood me and she knew her role was to remind me to stop yearning and start learning. Beating myself emotionally was par for the course. As confident and self-assured I was in the business world, my personal life was polar opposite. I needed to break the chains of indecision. The power to decouple my physiology from the birth error was within my grasp. All I had to do was follow the instructions I received today and wishing would become reality.

The evening passed slowly. I slept soundly for the first time in months. I had work to do to arrange every step in the surgical preparation process. I awoke the next morning at peace with myself. Another Autumn day broke over the horizon, struggling to push back the night. I felt the connection as I struggled to push the remnants of indecision and doubt over my emotional horizon.

As I showered I examined my body. I smiled at the thought of the penis being transformed into a vagina. I stifled the urge to speak a statement thanking it for its service, although it failed me at times as gender dysphoria took hold of me. It didn't matter. In a month I'd be over the breakwater and free to navigate my new biology.

Boarding the regional rail in Cornwell Heights I looked for my train buddy. She was knitting another beautiful article for her granddaughter. I sat beside her and we talked. When I told her about my upcoming surgery she beamed. My friend was so supportive. She was a role model for society! We talked until we reached our stop at Jefferson Station. When we disembarked, she hugged me. We hugged at the end of each week to send warm wishes to carry us until we saw each other again. This hug felt deeper and more emotional. She was truly happy for me and I loved her more for being non-judgmental, supportive and a strong and determined woman.

Walking to the office the day after my consult cum surgery commitment, I felt differently about life. This was going to be a game changer. I was going to be able to dismiss the feeling of being almost complete, almost female, almost home. I was going to be able to jettison all the special undergarments necessary to appear female below the waist. I was going to be liberated!

Pushing my way through the revolving door I greeted the lobby attendant at the front desk warmly. They were always so gracious and welcoming. It had been almost a year since I entered the building for the first time as my authentic self. If they knew, and it would be presumptuous to assume they didn't, their demeanor wasn't showing any aversions. The elevator ride was short and the car empty. Exiting on my floor I entered the suite and danced to my office. My heart was lighter now than it was when I entered the suite for the first time as my authentic self. I felt I could float away without a care or worry. I had accomplished the biggest success of my life, living my authentic self!

I made the circuit from office to kitchen, greeting the early arrivers individually. There were only a few hearty souls who made it in as early as I did. Carrying a steaming mug of coffee to my office I settled in front of my computer to start the day. In the back of my mind I was compiling a list of people to tell about surgery and my time away from the office. I had already groomed my staff to handle daily functions as independently as they felt comfortable. I served as a backstop for challenges or problems they weren't able to handle alone. I had put into place a strong and well-informed team. I had full faith and confidence that things would proceed in their capable hands and they would reach me in the event I needed to help get them past a sticking point. I would be only a phone call away.

By nine o'clock the office was in full swing. I spoke with each member of my team individually; announcing my first full vacation of the year followed by extended leave for a major essential surgical procedure. It was as if my announcement had been leaked to the press.

"Unofficial sources, speaking on the condition of anonymity, tell Transgender News that Nikki DiCaro, Senior Vice President has scheduled gender affirmation surgery on December 7, 2016. Our source was unwilling to reveal the name of the surgeon or the hospital where DiCaro will undergo the procedure."

My announcement was met with something less than enthusiasm. It was as if there was fear of legal action if the wrong question or questions was asked. I guess the age of innocence had been deconstructed; replaced by the age of caution. I refused to reveal the nature of the surgery. Nobody needed to know. It wasn't their business. But I could read the expression on their face. They knew what I wasn't telling them. Over the next month I was to learn they were also hiding something vital from me.

With that behind me I relaxed for a few moments before running down the list of things I needed to do to ensure I was going to be able to go through with the surgery that only months prior seemed to be beyond my ability to reconcile.

Chapter 6

No person is a failure as long as a person has friends. - Anonymous

Friends. Let's talk about friends. My "friend ship" sails smoothly through calm seas. It's the turbulent, churning seas of life that require all hands-on deck to navigate the boiling waters that represent life's challenges. We can attempt to navigate solo. I'll tell you that approach would be a fool's errand. We have this innate sense of self – bravado – the sense that we're invincible. But are we? Can we embrace solitude? Can solitary living enrich us? Does human interaction seem beyond reach or not something we count among the important elements of a full life?

I don't count myself among the people who can successfully go it alone. I need companionship. I cherish the closeness of friends who have room in their heart to carry some of the burdens that inconveniently weigh on my heart. During the period of my awakening, I discovered heart friends and sister friends. I found in others the characteristics that made connecting effortless. I found strength in others; strength in areas where I lacked. It's difficult to admit we're weak. We like to think of ourselves as complete; but we're not. There's nothing wrong with admitting our flaws. I know, we fear ridicule. "Let's not let anyone know we're vulnerable. We're already exposed by our gender dysphoria. We don't need another breach in our fissuring granite façade. We've already suffered enough by exposing our authenticity to ridicule, recrimination and worse!

I'm not that good. I'm not convinced of my invincibility. In fact, until I transitioned, I feared hiding my vulnerability was keeping me at arms' length from people who might be able to help me past whatever mental or emotional obstacle that appeared in my path. I think I feared opening up. I had a secret; a deep, dark secret. I think I was afraid I might say too much; tell a confidant what was churning inside. I might go too far and expose the soft underbelly that I kept protected behind a muscular frame and male machismo.

When I committed to come out for the first time, the first inner defensive wall crumbled. I was happy to haul off the debris and clear the pathway to self-realization. It was scary. I was never one to admit weakness - blood in shark-infested waters. I shook with the early onset of panic. Grabbing myself by the emotional shorthairs I stood before a mirror and talked myself back from the psychological abyss. This was a new experience – trusting someone with this secret. We all know the upshot of revealing a secret. We can't put the secret back in the box once it's out. Pandora has nothing on us.

My opening up, coming out, admitting what I was, started within a network of likeminded people and built from there. Yes, I felt vulnerable but I never felt violated. I felt exposed but was quickly assured I wasn't alone. Those words "You're not alone" became my rock, my backstop, my safety net.

I *wasn't* alone. There were hundreds of transgenders at my inaugural coming out; a bi-monthly event that was taking place long before my appearance on the scene. There's nothing more powerful than walking into a room and realizing there are others, many others, living the same experience. Because of the commonality of the journey, I was able to build an excellent support network within the transgender community. My inner circle of trusted friends is a small cadre but I would match them against any other community of support. I also have an incredible network among cisgender men and women. Sure, they don't understand why I'm experiencing this phenomenon. Regardless, they embraced me immediately. Throughout the coming out, I learned about myself and my ability to explain who I was; who I really was.

When I step back from my announcement, however I present it, I realize people really didn't know me the way they thought. This can be frightening. It can be too much too quickly. It can be too much, period! Maybe we set our expectations too high. We know us. We really know us. We need to realize we've lived with ourselves our entire life. Sounds obvious, right? It's true. We've wrestled the demons, fed the elephant hoping not to get trampled when it decided to move around the emotional room. Our intimacy, the familiarity of it, may cause us to overestimate acceptance. We're the same person inside. We're changing the exterior. It's that simple, right? Why would it be a big deal for anybody to grasp and embrace? It may be simple for us, a fait accompli, but it's traumatic for others. Not everyone, to be certain, but it is a major change. We look one way one day and differently another day. If we think that isn't a shock to the system, we should think again.

We sometimes expect too much too soon from too many. It's important we realize this is a cleansing process of sorts. Cleansing or purging of our base of friends, family and supporters; or people we thought were friends, family and supporters. Presenting people with something that falls like a ton of bricks crushing their boundary of reality can be unnerving and alienating. For those who come through these discussions feeling as close or closer than before we opened up to them, we marvel at the depth and breadth of feelings and emotions we share. The true friends, the real family and the unqualified supporters see past the façade, the box, and embrace the operating system. That's really who we are; the heart and soul of our being is the genuine us. If we understand humanity and all its frailties and misgivings and have good connective tissue with others, that connection will withstand turbulence of an initial shock. It's these connections that carry us through life's downs. It's easy to be around to enjoy the ups. Who wouldn't want to be part of a life that's on the upswing, where everything's rosy and peachy and all the other positives?

If you can't connect with people when times are good, either you have a problem enjoying success, or people who remain at a distance are jealous or introverted or unable to share your joy due to some internal dysfunction. Don't be surprised if jealousy rears its ugly head. We've all experienced it along our journey. Jealousy is the domain of the dysfunctional; the ones who can't or won't allow us the simple joy of discovery, self-love and emotional and psychological peace.

In the transgender community, we are complementary and we also contrast. It's the differences that bind us almost as much as the similarities. There are also latent issues that will surface from time to time. Building a trusted and loyal support group takes time, energy and discernment. We all trust and at times that trust will be betrayed. This is true in life generally and in any subset of society specifically. How we deal with betrayal will either weaken or strengthen us. That's why it's important to have a spectrum of friends. Because some will come and go. Not everyone who enters our life is destined to stay. Take what we can from them in terms of education and give back what we're capable of returning. When visitors depart, hopefully they won't leave an unfillable void.

    Think about our community; both personal and professional. We may consider it no surprise that a person has a good community of support. That's not a foregone conclusion. Things have to click. The universe has to intervene and most importantly, we need to be open to the messages coming our way. Building a community of support requires emotional and psychological investment. Success requires interdependence, bi-lateral acceptance and compromise. We determine the outskirts of these boundaries and whether we are willing to venture beyond those boundaries to welcome people into our inner sanctum.

    During gender transition it's all too easy to become self-absorbed, self-centered and insular. We don't really understand the vastness of our difference from conventional society. We don't know who to trust. That skepticism makes it all too easy to raise the drawbridge, fill the mote and arm the battlements. We can revert to a protectionist approach to the world. After all, haven't we hidden in plain sight all along?

    When I consider the vast difference between my former life and my current life I sometimes wonder how I was able to maintain my sanity. In my former life I felt stifled, boxed in by the insecurity of who I was and what I was. Naturally I thought this was my fate, my lot in life – to be different without knowing why. More importantly, I didn't realize I wasn't alone. I was going to have to sail through uncharted waters without the benefit of experienced, professional assistance. Who was I going to tell? What was I going to tell them? How crazy would my story sound? I maintained my secret; protected it like a treasure that weighed me down. It was too precious, too rare and too frightening to share. I protected it as if someone would steal it. I never considered the potential that if someone would steal this "thing" from me, snatch it like a thief, I might be freed from the burden, the yoke of being different.

    Although I tried many times to wish away my dysphoria, I was wrong. Not because I underestimated myself; it was easy to underestimate when the yoke of nonconformity weighed heavily upon me. One thing I learned, a difficult lesson, was that I underestimated the universe and its power. The path to the future was being carved out for me without my input or knowledge. That path included carrying gender dysphoria through to physical transition and emotional and psychological fulfillment. Since my transition, I've blossomed and have experienced a birth of social skills. I realized I would not be required to carry any burden too heavy for me to successfully overcome.

I have a powerful, supportive and loving network of friends. I'd like to take credit for the genesis of my network. Truthfully, it all started innocently when I summoned the courage to approach another transgender during my first night out as my authentic self at the beginning of 2013.

This was the proving ground, the practice, the confidence builder. My time to shine tolled in my mind. I had taken the leap of faith and dressed to express my true gender. But the courage wasn't imbedded in the clothing. The clothing, makeup and other accessories became my statement, my identifier. I was burnished. I courageously stepped out of the protective cocoon of my living quarters and into the public eye. This breach of secrecy, this bold action, this exposure to potential recriminations galvanized my desire to not travel alone.

I made my first friend on January 13, 2013. After that evening I opened the door to my heart just enough to allow the light from other hearts to break across my doorway and illuminate my path. This light conquered the shadows of worry that had cast long and heavy across the landscape of my life.

Friendship isn't for the faint of heart. It requires commitment, trust and ongoing effort to support. Friendship is not the destiny of every encounter. Discernment is critical to ensure our needs mesh with those who enter our life. Not everyone has the mojo to be our friend. And we may not have the mojo to be their friend. Friendship is a recipe and the people are the ingredients. Commonality of thought, belief, purpose and other relevant qualities define the fit and feel of potential friends. We may use the term "friend" loosely. But when it comes down to who we can look to for the depth of support that gets us over rough patches in life, there will be a select few who will answer the bell every time. This is mutually important. Inviting people into our life that do not create an unbreakable bond perform a disservice to us and them. Therefore, not every encounter results in friendship

I made many acquaintances. Some tried to blossom into friendship only to wither. That failure wasn't due to either of us lacking the desire for a relationship. We weren't destined to be friends. That's okay. Remember, we can only nurture, maintain and sustain a finite number of friends in the truest sense of the word. Those failures signified losing a turn, going back a space and becoming casual acquaintances. Those failures were not intended as a major setback in my journey to fulfillment. They were a very valuable learning experience.

Define what you want friendship to be. For me when it comes to friends, it's impossible to have many close friends. Friendship that connects to my heart demand these relationships be nurtured, cultivated, sustained and supported. Devoting time to establishing and maintaining connective emotional tissue is critical to sustaining deep and lasting friendships. These friendships are the essence of a quality support network. Sounds like a business evaluation, right? Well, paint the words with whatever colors you choose. The concept of nurturing is critical for my well-being and personal success.

My heart friends stand with me during tough times. As a transgender, tough times and challenges come often. It's not that I cannot handle the tough times alone; I'm strong physically and emotionally. But my emotional tanks have a finite capacity. When I have a strong and unrelenting community of support, I can maintain a healthy level of fuel in my emotional tanks for those times when I need to summon the juice to spray away the toxic effect of negativity. My tanks are usually filled to overflowing. When I deplete a tank, my heart friends instinctively know and will visit or call. Our connective tissue sends alerts across the miles and one calls another to drain the sediment and refill with fresh emotional energy. I will expound on the topic of friends in another installment of my rolling memoires.

Chapter 7

The timing of the surgery, around the December holidays, afforded the opportunity to celebrate my physical change and the spirit of the season simultaneously. My rebirth curiously paralleled the Christian celebration of birth. Friends planned to visit to provide emotional support as well as physical assistance. They began planning their visits once I announced surgery. Accepting help wasn't one of my strong points. I was always the one helping, supporting, energizing. I tried, in vain, to help them understand I was going to be fine. They didn't need to burden themselves by journeying to me and doing whatever it is that friends do when a friend is in need. They insisted and I welcomed their insistence. If you're smart, you don't ever turn away willing friends who encourage and support. There's nothing much better at providing a cure for what ails you than the love of good friends.

The advent of surgery gave me the opportunity to evaluate my situation. Every moment in my life has been under the microscope of doubt and second-guessing. When decisions create permanent impact and change, they have a way of lingering. In other words, they have a very long half-life.

The woman inside was beckoning me. She was reminding me that she was always there with me regardless of whether I acknowledged her presence. She was mostly patient; when she wasn't insistent on making her presence felt and embraced. Early in my life this was the most difficult thing to do. Who and what was this thought, this presence insinuating itself into my life? What was I to make of it? I had no reference point, no information, nobody to educate, support or comfort me. I pushed her deep into my psyche. But through the years she persisted. She knew the timetable, the game plan, the tipping point.

My journey, the journey that has carried me this far, started with an emotional epiphany; an awakening of sorts that began not during the age of enlightenment. The journey originated during the age of conformity. I did what I was told. I followed a leader, even when that leader was cutting a swath directly to the edge of the abyss. This was part of my upbringing, learned flaws or biases. Never question authority was the mantra that radiated from my house. I think my parents feared that if I started questioning others it might morph into questioning them.

I was born first; the oldest of three. The process began with pulling me from the perfectly safe; perfectly serene and perfectly incestuous womb. Forceps shaped my large head and guided my 9 plus pound girth into the world. Little did I know the future being planned and how greatly it would diverge from convention. Being first had its privilege. It also conveyed responsibility. The first born is the test case for parents; their inaugural journey down the unlit, unpaved path of parenthood and family.

I don't remember much about early childhood. What I do recall didn't leave me warm and fuzzy. Parents were all about dictating the right course; their course. There was nothing original unless I looked back to preceding generations. My parents did what their parents did. All the good intentions of the parenting sages and pundits couldn't come close to anticipating what was buried deep inside me.

When gender dysphoria surfaced for the first time I was scared. I had no idea what was causing the feeling of being mentally and emotionally disconnected from my physical gender. I looked like a boy but I felt like a girl. There could not have been anything more foreign than that. I knew I was experiencing feelings and emotions I dared not share. I couldn't share for many reasons, the most important was I didn't know what to call it or how to explain it. Besides, my parents would have had no clue what to do with me if I revealed I was harboring feelings of being a woman. They might think I was crazy.

"The kid's off his nut. Maybe he was dropped in the nursery. Maybe the forceps scrambled his brain. Maybe they gave us the wrong kid when we left the hospital."

I could imagine my parents running through all the possible reasons. They would be embarrassed. If I thought I was feeling unappreciated and misunderstood before I revealed my feminine tendencies, imagine how those fears would be redefined. Terror gripped me; forcing me to push femininity deep into my subconscious. I hid in plain view as I tried to assuage the need to express the girl inside. The energy I expended to repress the thoughts and feelings at times felt debilitating. Half of my energy was spent keeping my errant emotions and feelings in check leaving me with feelings of emptiness and longing for escape.

Chapter 8

We've all heard about the benefits of creating and maintaining a journal. It's cathartic, it helps to heal. Writing has opened my mind's eye to the possibilities life offers. These possibilities didn't always shout their existence. They resided among the flowers and the trees. They floated with the clouds. They may have rolled off the tip of the tongue of people who crossed my path. It's up to me to identify them and to reach for them. If they were meant for me they would respond to my advances. I had been writing for ten years. I wrote eleven fiction novels that included strong female characters. I lived vicariously through those females, unwittingly transferring my anxiety to them and allowing them to shoulder some of my burden.

I discovered the marvels of life when I followed the advice of a friend. She told me to stand with feet shoulder width apart, close my eyes, look up and raise my arms in the shape of a "V". She told me to hold that position for three minutes and the universe would come to me.

After three minutes, I can't tell you I felt any different. But something had been altered in my outlook. That day's actions changed the course of my life. I began to document my thoughts and feelings. I wrote a daily journal, two hundred twenty-five entries over the course of a year. Each entry ranged from 250 – 1,000 words. The experience was not only cathartic, but also enlightening. Everyone experiences doubt, second-guessing, uncertainty, regret. Writing feelings and thoughts can help us to cope with these emotions and overcome their potentially chilling, debilitating or regressive impact. Creating daily journals enabled me to maintain front of mind focus on my goals and objectives. In the face of potentially destructive backlash from self-centered, prejudicial, biased and bigoted people I encountered on the last miles of my journey towards transition. Credit for the inspiration to write must go to the powers of the universe.

I wrote poetry. My first poem defined the struggle and organized the confusing mass of emotions.

I met a girl I thought I knew before

Transcendence – My Rebirth as a Woman

She was standing, waiting at my door
I heard her breathe
I heard her knock

I ignored her, hoping she would go away
She wasn't what I wanted
Or what I needed
No not nearly enough to satisfy

I met a girl I thought I knew before
She was standing, waiting at my door
I heard her breathe
I heard her knock

I went about my business as if she didn't exist
Another day in life surrounded by mist
After years of searching wishing and hoping
Imagining myself in the body of another
I discovered the girl still waiting but older
The person I always was and always will be

Longing and yearning, pining and sobbing
I opened the door and walked into my life
I embraced myself and the healing began
It finally came, it was there all the time
My life finally makes sense

Let living commence
If only I knew, if only I knew
I would not have wasted all that time.

  This poem, written on the evening of January 25, 2015, opened the
emotional floodgates. Rain fell in silent torrents as my body wracked.
This was the breakthrough I needed to make the decision to begin hormone
therapy.

Emotions ran high and low in random patterns. Writing helped me to vent without doing something I would later regret. Once the problem was reduced to a Word document or handwritten, the demon was entombed. I felt liberated. As importantly, when I read what I wrote I felt calm; as if I had settled whatever issue had surfaced. I also realized how futile it would have been to confront the problem directly. The opportunity to set things right, to enjoy vindication, would come when the universe was prepared to permit it.

I understood that people who took potshots weren't worth my time to react or respond. Neither result would have done anything more than potentially enflame an already tense situation. So I took the high road and allowed detractors, of which there were only a few, to wallow in their narrow-minded world.

I leaned on friends. These influencers included people around me who were part of my inner circle. These were the people with whom I could express my authentic self without fear of recrimination, judgment or rejection. Were they always complimentary? Of course not. No true friend will always tell you what you want to hear. That's called pandering and pandering can be destructive by creating a false sense of security that is thinner than onion paper.

Even when situations made me tense and threatened to empty my emotional tanks, I chose to write positively. Writing negative thoughts would not serve to lift me or my readers. There was already too much negativity in life. I wasn't going to allow emotional down strokes to weigh on me. Being negative would be admitting I wasn't capable of handling my burden. Also, I would have to climb out of the emotional trough I had dug.

Here is another journal entry:

It's Over the Hump in Pumps Day! and with the warming trend pumps might be on the wardrobe menu. What shall we chat about today? Several topics come to mind. Lately I feel like I go to the language butcher. I listen to the news, participate in conversations and is it me or is our language being chopped to shreds? Maybe I'm too sensitive - a writer tends to be overly critical about literary things. I'll apply more baby powder, maybe that will help (wink, wink!!).

I smirk when I hear people say, "you better" this and "you better" that. Not sure where I lost control, or gave the impression that I can't make decisions for myself. Certainly (notice I didn't call you Shirley) I value input, suggestions and feedback. What bugs me is the "so self-assured" that only they know what's best. Experience that in your life? Yeah, yeah, I know this sounds like a downer - it's not meant to be. Rather I want to point out that at no juncture in our lives should we eh-ver turn the controls over to another. We may allow certain people to exercise influence, adjust our route of flight, fine tune our trajectory, but ceding control? I'm not so sure about that. Recall this is your life we're talking about. You'll listen to opinions, solicit feedback, process and decide.

How do you bask in the glow of success if that success is not yours? We need successes, large and small, to keep the mental strings tight, the emotional pistons pumping, the crank shaft of discernment turning clockwise.

Turn on the filter, keep it clean and clear. Don't let it get clogged by overbearing insistences. Every day is a new day and every day is a challenge. Minimize or eliminate the things that don't add value, that keep you from completing your mission, achieving your goals, reaching each day's finish line.

You are unique and we want you to stay that way because your uniqueness adds value to every life you touch.

A big part of the self-discovery process involves coming out from behind the birth façade. This was painful for me. I had lived more than half a century in my birth gender. I raised four children, hired many hundreds of people, built professional and personal relationships, bought and sold properties and built a nest egg for retirement. I attended grade school, high school and college. I made friends, some of which continue. I built a solid and formidable history. History can be rewritten but at what investment and to what end?

Sure, I struggled under the yoke of my life's work. It's impossible to traverse this many years and not leave permanence in my wake. Permanence, the word can strike fear into the hearts of even the most ardent of change agents. Each year of life lived strengthens the headwinds that buffet change. The ghost of bygone days can haunt mercilessly and relentlessly. A person can be mired in the past. Not only haunted by regrets of things undone, risks not taken, opportunities lost, but anchored as if in cement shoes, to life already lived.

I'm not advocating forsaking the past. The past provides a certain layer of definition. The past may underpin our ability to move forward. We choose to add layers to our past or we try to erase vivid yet unflattering memories. Those memories may be relegated to the back of a mental file drawer deep in the recesses of our subconscious. But they will always be there. And some artifact may surface at inopportune times. Remember, the past has been lived. Rehashing the past as if we were required to relive it and live within its walls, limits our abilities by whatever delimiters we allow the past to construct. Living in the past means being a permanent resident of Reminiscenceville. Borrowing a line from an old movie I reconstitute it this way:

I coulda been a contenda, I coulda been a somebody. Instead I bought myself a one-way ticket to Reminiscenceville.

Weaker people succumb to such headlong assaults. I guess history serves a higher purpose in addition to paving the way for our future. History is a teacher and an educator. If we permit it to rule us, it can attach drag lines or anchors to our momentum; causing us to look back and yearn.

Look back at history to learn, never to yearn. – Nikki DiCaro

I chose to make history my friend rather than my nemesis and I was be able to improve upon my lot, my situation and steer a course for success and well-being.

The transition process isn't all about the person. There's no self-aggrandizement here. There is only self-expression, freeing me from the yoke of the identity that served to not only stifle me but to imprison me. I could have felt shackled to something that hindered my well-being. Three square meals of conventionality.

"Here, eat this porridge and drink the drink, it will keep you from thinking and living outside your comfort zone."

These aren't the words the world uses. But the actions and reactions of the world generally are to put people in categories; in the slow lane to the world's definition of normalcy.

I, by my struggle to break artificial molds and tear down artificial boundaries, am redefining normalcy. Every movement in my transition was similar to each click of the roller coaster as it ascended to the zenith, the crest of the hill. Tension built with each inch of progress. Exhilaration, excitement, trepidation, stress and anticipation sharpened my emotions. I knew I couldn't continue the journey without revealing my authentic self. The journey was mostly about me; although I've experienced thoughtless people trying to make the journey about them.

"Don't you realize you're going to make [insert name or description] unhappy if you do this? They're not going to be happy about you."

I've heard those words ad nauseam. I finally stood up (no I didn't rush to the window and fling it open) and said "Don't you think it's about time I was happy? I've spent my life making other people happy. It's my time now." The look on the other person's face was almost indescribable. As if they experienced an epiphany. They hadn't given one iota of thought to my happiness. This may sound harsh and impersonal. There's nothing impersonal about standing up for yourself. I didn't do that enough in ways that were logical and expressed in a civil tone. Transition is so personal, laying myself bare before others unsure how they would react; risking my well-being and credibility.

Coming out is a tough concept for people to grasp. There seems to be confusion as to why now; why not earlier or later. I've heard "why would you ever want to make this choice?" This is a tough concept to get across to some people. It gets harder when you get "Why are you doing this to me?" I stifled a "Get over yourself" response, trying to retain some modicum of self-control. Some people thought being female was a choice I made. I explained in as much detail as they could grasp, this wasn't a choice.

We reach the tipping point; I did. I could no longer wait; I couldn't. My true self reached the breaking point and refused to be ignored or rebuffed any longer; that was me to the letter. I knew I couldn't continue to lie to others but more importantly, to myself. I couldn't look myself in the eye and play the charade, the game, any longer. I had to confront the demons, the elephant in the room; footsteps forever pounding as the pachyderm marched through my consciousness. I needed to acknowledge to myself that others must be told. We wax and wane between telling and just letting people find out. The emotional cost of going back and forth across the gender continuum is expensive and verges on debilitating.

Coming out is a personal thing; a unique experience. There's no script, no prerecorded transmission, no book of successful phrases, anecdotes, pithy statements. Nothing prepared me for this moment. I talked with professionals – therapists, psychologists, etc. – and other people who successfully transitioned. They were only be able to provide guidance. Since this was my journey, I worked hard and long to ensure coming out wouldn't be my Waterloo.

I battled insecurities and uncertainties. I struggled with who to tell, how to tell them and how to protect myself if they reacted badly. The human element within each person on my list of "the people I must tell" provided the backdrop of unwelcome suspense. Although I felt relief over finally shedding the male façade that became too heavy and cumbersome to carry, thinking about telling people about the real me wasn't always enjoyable. I didn't cherish this part of the journey. I didn't look forward to 'spilling the beans'. I worried they would have been overcooked and trampled by the mad rush to escape my presence. I attempted to handicap each outcome by gauging each recipient's emotional intelligence. I guessed correctly some of the time. But there were unwelcome surprises. I experienced them and they were momentarily painful. I didn't expect all people to understand.

I didn't expect everyone I told to wrap me in a warm, congratulatory embrace. It's not possible and it's unrealistic to expect everyone to embrace this change. It can be traumatic for some, an 'ah ha moment' for others. And for another subset it might be a non-event. "What you're doing does affect me one bit. So why should I care?"

Some people embraced me immediately. They were 'over the moon' for me. The depth of their support reassured me. I analyzed the successes and the failures during this part of the journey. I felt calm settle over me. I compared that calm to the feeling of standing outside during a quiet and steady snow fall. No wind, no turbulence; only soft white flakes floating. The air smelled clean with winter's crispness. The world was at peace if only for a brief period and so was I.

We all need reassurance, no matter how strong we think we are. I thought I was strong. Coming out tested my mettle. Some people purportedly close to me feigned shock or dismay. I was embraced by some blood relatives, disowned by a few. A few even told me I offended them and because of my problem they didn't want to know me any longer. I wasn't surprised but I was hurt. For my detractors, no amount of prior goodwill, prior financial or emotional support or unconditional love assured that certain members of my immediate family would tolerate me if not welcome me.

I began to think maybe I was adopted. "Mom, please tell me the truth. I was adopted, right? It won't kill me to know." I paused. "I'm so different from everyone in this family. I feel like I don't belong. Tell me I'm adopted and it will help me understand why I don't fit in here." I spoke in a calm and reassuring tone. I was hoping she would say something, anything. Instead she sat in the recliner and stared straight ahead. I wondered if she was confirming my suspicions by her inaction.

The problem with some people is lack of emotional bandwidth. For others, the problem is bias, prejudice and bigotry. These are all learned character flaws. It's impossible to unlearn lifetime experiences in a moment. For some people, clinging to their beliefs, no matter how flawed, becomes their safe harbor. I wondered who these detractors were. I thought I knew them. Obviously, I didn't know them at all. Being abandoned by people I thought I could trust was the equivalent of the brick of reality smacking me in the head. Sadly, emotional intelligence is only one element of the multivariate human equation that could have left me banged up and broken.

External influences complicate matters. The people I was preparing to tell may be their own person; willing to accept my story on its merits. In many cases these people are influenced by spouse, parents, children, in-laws, friends, beliefs, fears, insecurities and other intangibles that mold their perspectives. Blood relations didn't assure me of any measure of success. I worked to craft my message, careful to avoid apologies, flagging confidence and excuses. Any sign of weakness in my resolve would have fueled uncertainty not only in me but also in the people I told. They examined every aspect of my delivery. I wondered if I was confident enough. Was my body language consistent with my words?

Did I practice my delivery enough to ensure consistency? How many times did I practice before felt ready? Each time I caught a flaw in my delivery it threatened to delay coming out. Avoidance becomes my adversary because if I embraced 'avoidance' as an ally I would have betrayed myself. Waiting can become a millstone growing heavier daily. But I couldn't throw caution to the wind and appear as my authentic self without warning. Shocking people by presenting as my authentic self without warning would have been psychological suicide. I would have been viewed as unstable, not trustworthy, insecure, mentally unbalanced. And I would have forfeited any opportunity for success.

Unfortunately, even with ample preparation and self-confidence there was no guarantee my journey to authenticity would be smooth and enjoyable. I built courage with confidence. I knew I had no choice but to reveal this part of myself that nobody knew except me. Maybe some anticipated there was something going on that wasn't within their range of normalcy. I had to make peace with the knowledge that transitioning to live as my authentic self was the first step; a huge step. Transitioning isn't about meeting other people's expectations. This is my life, my feelings, my emotions and most of all my well-being. Telling people about the real me was monumental and absolutely essential. There was no way I could live another day as my former self; behind the façade that restrained my authenticity, my energy and my creativity.

The plan was well thought out, vetted with my friends and tested with people who I knew would be open to my transition. They encouraged me and joined my network. They were happy for me; overjoyed and humbled by the fact that I trusted them enough to share my deepest secret. Because of the planning, and the good relationship I had developed with the people in my sphere of influence, acceptance was better than I anticipated.

I was nervous and it almost overwhelmed my confidence. If you want a dose of reality to confirm the difficulties of being who you are without apology, without regret and with the conviction that you have the inalienable right to life, liberty and the pursuit of happiness, read the following journal entry.

I had the privilege to attend a play called The Laramie Project at Steel River Playhouse in Pottstown, PA. I had recently joined the board of directors of the LGBT Equality Alliance, based in Chester County, PA. The board asked if I would sub for the organization's founder at the showing and facilitate / moderate a talk back between the audience and the cast after the performance. The Laramie Project presented the life of Matthew Shepard, cut tragically short by his beating death; a hate crime for the sole reason he was an out and proud gay teen attending college in Laramie, Wyoming. I had never heard of Matthew Shepard. He died in 1998 while I was steeped in my business career prior to the advent of the new century and all of the dread about the end of the world at the turn of the century.

I was given a complimentary ticket for agreeing to facilitate the talk back. When I entered the small theater, I was greeted warmly by a volunteer who asked my seat number. I had presumed seating was similar to a movie theater. I extracted the ticket from the right pocket of my mauve suede jacket and handed it over. She smiled, announced the seat row and number and pointed me in the right direction.

The row letters were written on labels and affixed inconsistently on the outer leg of the end seat. I was destined for row C and when I climbed to the third row I searched for seat numbers. There was one open seat at the end of the row. I looked across the row to count the seats. The soft eyes of a man seated to the left of the open seat beckoned me to ask, "What is your seat number?" He smiled and announced "nine."

"Then this must be seat ten!" I smiled warmly and settled into the chair.

"What's your name?" My theater buddy asked.

"I'm Nikki. Nikki, one "N", two "K"s and two "I"s but no "C". He offered his hand gently. I shook it.

"Nice to meet you Nikki. I'm Andrew."

"Hello Andrew." I paused. "What do you do for a living?" Old habits of stale ice breakers were difficult to lose.

"I work in Philadelphia." I wasn't sure if my question felt intrusive. Undeterred I continued. "Public sector or private?"

"The woman in row B turned and smiled. Andrew looked at her. Are we public or private?"

"Government," she announced.

"Oh, the third form."

"Third?" He asked.

"Public, private and government," I replied.

Andrew and his friend in row B smiled. "This is my new friend Nikki." Andrew introduced me. I'm terrible with names and can't recall the smiling woman's name. She turned and contributed to our conversation. It was comfortable and later I learned it was destiny's design that Row C Seat 10 was designated for me.

"Where do you live?" Another stock question from my inane repertoire of queries.

"Philadelphia."

"Where in Philadelphia?" I was beginning to feel like I was probing in a sensitive area. Andrew answered and then asked the same of me.

"Centreville, Maryland."

"Centreville?" He asked as if he knew this 1794 vintage enclave.

"Yes, do you know it?"

"I live in Chestertown. About four miles closer to you than the town."

"Wow!" I thought of the possibilities that I would be placed in a seat next to someone three and one half hours north of home and a stone's throw from mine. Coincidence? I think not. Given how my life has played out since my physical transition, there's design. I'd expand by adding the word "intelligent" but that would spark debate and possibly castigation from intelligent design proponents. This we'll save for another day and another time.

We exchanged contact information at intermission. As we enjoyed the second half of the performance I cried and Andrew seemed to feel my pain and empathize. He had seen the plot twice, I believe, yet was drawn to it again. Given what little I knew of my most recent friend, I presumed there was something deep and abiding in the message.

The performers (I wouldn't consider them actors as they seemed to live the multiple parts each thespian was chosen to portray) delivered the message in character. They depicted the response of each interviewee whose life Matthew had touched. These individual character performances were based on the results of interviews conducted during two trips to Laramie over a two-year period. I was visibly moved by the depth of conviction of each character's presentation of the senseless loss of life of an eighteen-year-old college student for living his life true to his sexuality. He was robbed of the opportunity, to flourish and continue to contribute to society, by two young men who thought they would lure Matthew away and beat him into changing him to their narrow view of life.

Maybe there are those who would offer that the destructive duo went too far by killing Matthew. That would be blatantly wrong. They went too far by believing that might makes right and attacking a person, in any way, shape or form, is the appropriate human response to someone who is diverse. Matthew's budding life was cut short; a rose bud snipped from the bush just as all of spring's promise was about to burst forth in the rose's blossoming. Justice was served (two young men adjudicated to prison for the remainder of their lives), albeit too late. One of the messages from the play was remembrance. We must learn from tragedy and strive to never repeat it. The destruction of lives, Matthew's and the two killers, their families, friends, the town of Laramie and anyone who was touched by the wanton disregard for human life, is never worth the lessons learned.

It's too late when we're holding vigils, commemorations, remembrances, etc. We can't undo what's been done. We need to overcome the need to categorize, criticize, analyze, ostracize, victimize and every other negative "ize" that exists now and in the future.

Matthew's tragically shortened life leaves us empty and robbed of the richness he would have added; as does any tragically shortened life. We have a tendency to become guarded, to nurture bias, to feel uncomfortable. These negative occurrences paint good people with the brush of generalization which further deepens divides, stifles healing, foments mistrust and fuels the potential for more hatred and destruction.

When will it end? Given the apparent lack of compassion, not soon enough.

The Laramie Project affirmed the difficulties of living my authentic self. I already knew there would be headwinds buffeting my journey. My transition was successful. Nothing would ever influence me to retrace my path. I am living loud and proud of who I am. I know why I am and will continue to be me regardless of the blowback, or rejection. Fortunately, there are more pockets of acceptance than rejection. It is sad that the unconventional, like me, must evaluate every situation to determine if we risk our lives by being our authentic self wherever we travel.

I end this segment of my memoirs with two blog posts that helped keep my course steady.

Good morning girls; Tremendous Tuesday. Well it would have to be if it followed Marvelous Monday! Lots going on today. Work is busy and keeping me focused away from show sales and dress sales and panty sales... well you get the idea. Recalling the crowd at Keystone it struck me that our little unconventional economy is not so little. We're not only a movement, we are the entire symphony.

Remember that. Remember you have the ability to play whatever melody you like. Enjoy the give and take; the crescendo and the fortissimo. Be heavy metal or jazz, be classical or contemporary. Don't just be notes on a scale.

Add your words, sing out loud!

Live life and enjoy it!

Happy over the hump day. The day is shaping up to be a beauty, just like all of you. Mother Nature has nothing on us. Her natural beauty pales in comparison to you, my sisters.

Thursday in the City of Sisterly Love brings anticipation for another fine weekend of fun as the laptop lounge heads to August Moon. We had sisters from as far west as Harrisburg, as far south as Baltimore, as far north as Rutherford, New Jersey and as far east as Whiting, New Jersey (I'm sure I missed a place so forgive the lack of thorough coverage) bringing smiles, hugs and wonderful personalities to make last Saturday's event a smashing success.

It's so good to see everyone and it begs the question of whether we should augment these gatherings with a daylong event. I'm sure we can cobble together a group and plan a day of being out and about.

Spring is almost here and I'm so excited! Strip off that overcoat and bring out the soft pastels and light and airy outfits.

Sister Spring has wheeled old man winter to the rest home. He may try for one last hurrah but it's going to be too little too late. Pack your cares away, polish up those apples, energize that smile and let's see the twinkle in your eyes dance playfully as you prepare for another relaxing and enjoyably feminine weekend.

Have a feline ferocious and femininely fulfilling day.

Transcendence continues with Book Two – Turning into Second Fiddle.

The journey continues with an excerpt from Book Two:

When I completed the coming out portion of my transition, I found several people in my organization who weren't willing to accept me. I tried to understand the reasons for the rejection. They left me to try to figure out their mental or emotional immaturity. The response was the same; "I don't have a problem with transgenders." I wondered whether these people were attempting to convince me or convince themselves. I decided the problem was theirs to own and operate. If they couldn't come around to realizing that everything wasn't black and white, why would I want to waste time and energy trying to convince them?

The phenomenon of control transference occurred once I presented as my authentic self. Transference of dominance from male to female and taking my not-do-rightful place among weaker sex, the submissive gender, the feminine members of society whose work is never done.

The dominant male syndrome was alive and well but I no longer was a member of the fraternity. I had surrendered my membership to the boys' club. But I was never a charter member. I always felt distant, disconnected. I did what I was expected to do. After I did it enough it became unconscious action.

The influence I wielded as the male boss dissipated when I presented as a woman. In meetings, men talked over me and interrupted me. There were apologies sprinkled onto my ego like so many tasteless seasonings. The assault continued. What was once, acceptance of ideas and discourse around them morphed into, "That sounds interesting but let's ask [insert name], I think he's got a better idea." All dismissals were offered with a smile that hid contempt for my transition.

It was a large and bitter pill to swallow. Every decision, indecision, action and inaction carries consequences. In order to be happy I needed to sacrifice something. In my prior gender expression, I could be authoritative and unflinching in my expectations. I could act like I was part of the dominant component of society. I guess what goes around comes around. I wasn't happy with myself; the inner woman struggling behind the façade of my birth gender. I compensated by overexpressing myself. I think that's called hyper masculinity.

To get what I wanted and to be where I desired to be, I was willing to compromise. I didn't realize how deep and wide the chasm between where I was and where I wanted to be. I was no longer that hard-charging man. I was that bitchy, difficult woman who insisted on having things her way! Maybe I hadn't learned to finesse my way around obstacles. I was strong. I wasn't going to spend time digging pathways and hacking through bramble to work around a problem. I was a conqueror. Defeat the dragon and you never have to wonder when it will flame you into a charred mass.

Finesse is a finely tuned skill with its roots in artful leadership. This is something we can teach men and women. I believe we can capitalize on the plethora of research and conclusions about this phenomenon and coach the business world into seeing men and women through one professional, unbiased lens. There is bias, deep-rooted and unconscious. By definition, unconscious bias occurs automatically as does about 95% of our actions and reactions.

Transcendence – Turing into Second Fiddle. Coming to Amazon and Kindle Direct. If you would like to receive an update when Book Two becomes available, please visit my website and subscribe to updates.

I hope you enjoyed the first installment of my memoirs. Please continue to follow my journey.

Thank you - Nikki

Nikki DiCaro

References:

[i] Landau, J. (April 19, 1969). "James Taylor". Rolling Stone. Retrieved 2014-04-05.
[ii] Farber, B.A. (2007). *Rock 'n' Roll Wisdom: What Psychologically Astute Lyrics Teach about Life and Love*. Greenwood Publishing. p. 13. ISBN 9780275991647.

Made in United States
North Haven, CT
09 November 2023